Meditation and the Path to Self-Discovery

Meditation and the Path to Self-Discovery

Connecting with Your True Essence

Evangeline Brooks

Mindful Pages

Published in 2023

ISBN: 9789358814958 (PB)
ISBN: 9789358814828 (eBook)

Published by

Mindful Pages
Imprint of Alpha Editions LLC
312 W. 2nd St #1834
Casper, WY 82601, USA

Contents

Introduction

In the hustle and bustle of our modern world, where the cacophony of daily life often drowns out the whispers of our inner selves, there exists a profound yearning—a yearning to uncover the profound truth that lies at the core of our being. We search for meaning amidst the chaos, reaching out for something that resonates with our deepest essence. This book, "Meditation and the Path to Self-Discovery: Connecting with Your True Essence," is a journey into the heart of this yearning, an exploration of the timeless wisdom that can lead us back to ourselves.

In our quest for self-discovery, we are like travelers on an ancient and winding path, obscured by the thickets of distraction, doubt, and disconnection. Yet, at the core of our being, there exists a wellspring of tranquility and wisdom that has been waiting patiently for us to return. It is a place where we can find solace amidst the chaos, clarity within the confusion, and a profound sense of purpose that transcends the ephemeral distractions of the modern world.

Meditation, the ancient art of inner contemplation, is the key that unlocks this hidden treasure within us. It is a practice that has been revered and embraced by sages, mystics, and seekers of truth throughout the ages. Through the simple act of turning inward, we can embark on a transformative journey that takes us beyond the superficial layers of existence and into the depths of our soul.

This book is an invitation to embark on that journey. It is a guide that will lead you through the labyrinth of your mind, helping you discover the profound stillness that exists beneath the surface of your thoughts and emotions. It will introduce you to the transformative power of mindfulness, compassion, and self-inquiry—tools that will help you navigate the complexities of your inner landscape.

As we delve into the realms of meditation and self-discovery, we will unravel the mysteries of the mind and heart, explore the science behind the practice, and hear the inspiring stories of individuals who have embarked on this path and emerged with a profound sense of purpose, peace, and inner harmony. We will learn how to connect with our true essence, how to listen to the whispers of our soul, and how to navigate the challenges of life with grace and resilience.

So, if you are ready to embark on a journey of self-discovery, if you are eager to reconnect with your true essence and find the answers that lie within, then turn the page and begin this transformative adventure. The path may be winding, and the terrain may be unfamiliar, but with each step, you will come closer to the timeless truth that resides at the core of your being—the truth that you are more than your thoughts, more than your emotions, and more than the external world would have you believe. You are a seeker of wisdom, a traveler of the soul, and this book is your guide on the path to self-discovery.

Part I: Foundations of Meditation

In the depths of every individual lies a profound yearning—a yearning to unravel the enigma of self, to grasp the essence of existence, and to fathom the purpose of life. This yearning is the flame that fuels the human spirit, propelling us to seek beyond the surface of our everyday existence and venture into the vast expanses of our inner worlds. Embarking on a journey of self-discovery is an odyssey of introspection and transformation, a voyage into the core of our being where we unearth the raw beauty and wisdom that reside within.

The journey of self-discovery is akin to setting sail on an uncharted sea, where the waters may be turbulent and the winds unpredictable. It's a journey that demands courage, vulnerability, and an open heart. It's an expedition that necessitates shedding the layers of societal conditioning, external expectations, and false identities we may have adopted over time. To embark on this voyage, we must be willing to confront our fears, face our shadows, and embrace our authenticity.

Meditation, the compass for this expedition, guides us through the ebbs and flows of our inner voyage. It's the practice that enables us to silence the cacophony of the external world and tune into the symphony of our soul. Through meditation, we cultivate the art of mindful presence, allowing us to observe our thoughts without judgment, to explore our emotions with compassion, and to witness the subtle whispers of our true selves.

As we navigate this journey, we encounter our beliefs, both empowering and limiting. We confront the narratives that have shaped our perceptions, the beliefs that have defined our actions, and the stories that have written the script of our lives. Self-discovery invites us to question these beliefs, to discern their origins, and to consciously choose the ones that align with our authentic selves.

The journey of self-discovery is not a linear path; it's a labyrinth of experiences, introspection, and growth. Along the way, we stumble upon our strengths and weaknesses, our virtues and vices. We learn to celebrate our strengths and harness them to manifest our dreams, and we acknowledge our weaknesses, transforming them into opportunities for growth and self-improvement.

In the depths of our souls, we also discover our purpose—an essential compass guiding our journey. Purpose is the North Star that illuminates our path, providing clarity in times of confusion and motivation in moments of doubt. It's the force that propels us forward, urging us to make a meaningful impact on the world and to leave a legacy that transcends our existence.

Through the journey of self-discovery, we connect with the very essence of humanity, recognizing the interconnectedness of all beings. We cultivate compassion, empathy, and a deep appreciation for the diversity of human experiences. This understanding fosters a sense of unity and promotes kindness, love, and understanding in our interactions with others.

In conclusion, embarking on a journey of self-discovery is an invitation to peel back the layers of conditioning and delve into the depths of our true selves. It's a transformative expedition that unfurls the tapestry of our being, revealing the brilliance and authenticity that reside within. This voyage is not just an individual quest; it's a collective awakening—a reminder that in understanding ourselves, we contribute to a more enlightened and compassionate world. So, let us set sail on this journey, embracing the unknown, and discovering the boundless beauty of our true essence.

The Essence of Meditation

The essence of meditation lies in the profound art of turning inward, transcending the noise of the external world, and immersing oneself in a state of profound presence and awareness. At its core, meditation is a practice that nurtures the mind, body, and spirit, offering a wide array of benefits for holistic well-being.

Stillness and Presence: Meditation is a practice of cultivating stillness in the mind. It's about learning to be fully present in the current moment, letting go of the past and future, and embracing the now.

In this state of profound presence, one can experience a sense of calm, peace, and inner tranquility.

Awareness and Mindfulness: Through meditation, individuals develop heightened awareness and mindfulness. This means attuning to one's thoughts, emotions, and bodily sensations without judgment. It's about observing the fluctuations of the mind and emotions like an impartial witness.

Stress Reduction: Meditation is a powerful tool for stress reduction. By calming the mind and activating the relaxation response in the body, it helps lower stress hormones like cortisol. Regular meditation practice can lead to reduced anxiety, improved emotional regulation, and better stress management.

Clarity and Insight: Meditation often leads to moments of profound clarity and insight. By quieting the mental chatter, individuals can gain a deeper understanding of themselves, their thought patterns, and the nature of reality. This insight can lead to personal growth and self-discovery.

Emotional Well-Being: Meditation can enhance emotional well-being by promoting positive emotions like gratitude, compassion, and joy. It also helps individuals navigate challenging emotions with greater ease, fostering emotional resilience.

Focus and Concentration: Meditation strengthens the mind's ability to focus and concentrate. It enhances attention span and cognitive function, making it a valuable tool for improving productivity and problem-solving.

Self-Compassion: Meditation encourages self-compassion and self-acceptance. It helps individuals develop a kinder and more compassionate relationship with themselves, reducing self-criticism and negative self-talk.

Connection and Unity: Some forms of meditation aim to deepen one's sense of interconnectedness with all of existence. This can lead to feelings of unity, empathy, and a sense of oneness with the world and its inhabitants.

Physical Health: Meditation has been linked to improved physical health. It can lower blood pressure, boost the immune system, and promote overall well-being. Some meditation practices, like mindfulness-based stress reduction (MBSR), are even used as complementary therapies in healthcare settings.

Spiritual Exploration: For many, meditation is a spiritual practice that connects them with a higher sense of purpose or the divine. It can be a vehicle for exploring questions of existence, meaning, and the nature of reality.

In essence, meditation is a versatile and deeply transformative practice that empowers individuals to explore the inner landscapes of their minds, find serenity in the midst of life's challenges, and nurture a greater sense of self-awareness and compassion. It is not a one-size-fits-all endeavor, as there are various forms and techniques, but the common thread is the journey inward toward a deeper understanding of oneself and one's connection to the universe.

Defining meditation and its significance

Meditation is a multifaceted practice that encompasses a wide range of techniques and approaches, but at its core, it can be defined as a deliberate and systematic mental exercise aimed at cultivating a state of heightened awareness, inner calm, and focused attention. It involves directing one's attention inward, often by concentrating on a particular object, thought, or sensation, or by simply observing the mind and its activities without attachment or judgment.

The significance of meditation lies in its potential to positively impact various aspects of an individual's life, including mental, emotional, physical, and even spiritual well-being. Here are key elements that highlight the significance of meditation:

> **Stress Reduction**: One of the most well-documented benefits of meditation is its ability to reduce stress. By calming the mind and relaxing the body, meditation helps lower stress hormones, promoting a sense of tranquility and emotional stability.

Improved Mental Health: Meditation can enhance mental health by reducing symptoms of anxiety and depression. It provides individuals with tools to manage racing thoughts and negative emotions, fostering emotional resilience.

Enhanced Concentration and Focus: Regular meditation practice can improve attention span and concentration. It teaches the mind to stay present, which can boost productivity and creativity.

Emotional Regulation: Meditation helps individuals become more aware of their emotions and develop healthier ways of responding to them. It encourages a mindful approach to emotions, reducing impulsive reactions.

Self-Awareness: Meditation fosters self-awareness by encouraging introspection and self-reflection. It allows individuals to explore their inner thoughts, feelings, and motivations, leading to greater self-understanding.

Physical Health Benefits: Meditation has been associated with several physical health benefits, such as lower blood pressure, improved immune function, and better sleep. It can be used as a complementary practice to support overall health.

Enhanced Relationships: Meditation can improve relationships by promoting empathy, compassion, and effective communication. When individuals are more centered and less reactive, their interactions with others tend to be more harmonious.

Spiritual Exploration: For those on a spiritual journey, meditation can be a profound tool for exploring questions of existence, the nature of consciousness, and the interconnectedness of all life. It can provide a sense of purpose and connection to something greater than oneself.

Mind-Body Connection: Meditation emphasizes the mind-body connection, highlighting how mental well-being can impact physical health. Techniques like mindfulness meditation encourage individuals to pay attention to bodily sensations and promote overall wellness.

Long-Term Well-Being: The benefits of meditation often extend beyond the immediate practice, contributing to long-term well-being. Regular meditators may experience a lasting sense of calm, increased resilience to life's challenges, and an improved overall quality of life.

In summary, meditation is a transformative practice that offers many benefits for individuals seeking greater well-being and self-discovery. Its significance lies in its ability to cultivate mindfulness, reduce stress, improve mental and emotional health, and promote a deeper understanding of oneself and the world. Whether approached as a secular tool for stress reduction or as a spiritual path, meditation holds the potential to enhance the quality of life and contribute to personal growth and self-realization

Historical roots and cultural perspectives

The practice of meditation has deep historical roots and has evolved within various cultural contexts over millennia. Its history is rich and diverse, shaped by the beliefs, philosophies, and traditions of different societies. Here, we'll explore the historical roots and cultural perspectives of meditation across some key civilizations:

Ancient India:

Vedic Period (1500-500 BCE): The earliest recorded mentions of meditation can be found in the Vedas, ancient Indian scriptures. During this period, meditation was primarily a religious practice aimed at connecting with the divine and understanding the nature of reality.

Upanishads (800-200 BCE): Meditation evolved further in the Upanishadic period, where it was explored as a means to achieve spiritual realization and transcendence. The concept of "Dhyana" (meditation) began to take shape.

Buddhism (6th century BCE): Siddhartha Gautama, who later became the Buddha, played a significant role in popularizing meditation. The Buddha's teachings emphasized mindfulness and insight meditation (Vipassana) as a path to enlightenment and the cessation of suffering.

Ancient China:

Taoism (6th century BCE): Taoist philosophy incorporated meditation as a means to align with the Tao, the fundamental principle underlying the universe. Taoist meditation practices aimed to cultivate inner harmony, longevity, and a deep connection with nature.

Confucianism: While Confucianism primarily focused on ethics and social order, meditation was also practiced to cultivate inner virtues and moral integrity.

Ancient Greece and Hellenistic Period (4th century BCE - 4th century CE):

Greek philosophers like Pythagoras and Plato explored meditation-like practices to seek wisdom, self-knowledge, and understanding of the cosmos. The term "philosophia" itself, meaning love of wisdom, reflects this quest for self-discovery.

Buddhism's Spread in Asia:

As Buddhism spread across Asia, it influenced and integrated with various cultures. In Tibet, for example, it gave rise to Tibetan Buddhist meditation practices like Vajrayana and Mahamudra.

In Japan, Zen Buddhism emphasized meditation as the central practice (zazen) and had a profound impact on Japanese culture and art.

Islamic Mysticism (Sufism):

Sufism, the mystical branch of Islam, incorporates various forms of meditation, such as Dhikr (remembrance of God), to seek closeness to the Divine and spiritual enlightenment.

Christianity:

Christian mystics, such as the Desert Fathers and St. John of the Cross, engaged in contemplative practices akin to meditation. These practices aimed to deepen one's relationship with God and achieve spiritual union.

Modern Western Adoption:

Meditation practices from various Eastern traditions gained popularity in the West during the 20th century. Figures like Paramahansa Yogananda and the Beatles helped introduce meditation to Western audiences.

Secular mindfulness meditation, derived from Buddhist Vipassana, became widely popular in the West, especially in clinical settings and for stress reduction.

Contemporary Global Perspectives:

Today, meditation is practiced worldwide in diverse forms. Mindfulness, Transcendental Meditation (TM), and yoga-based meditation are just a few examples of how meditation has adapted to contemporary life and culture.

Scientific research on meditation's benefits, particularly in fields like psychology and healthcare, has further globalized its practice.

In summary, meditation has a long and diverse history that spans across cultures and time periods. While it may have originated in specific religious and philosophical contexts, it has evolved and adapted to meet the needs of various cultures and individuals. Whether pursued for spiritual enlightenment, self-improvement, stress reduction, or personal growth, meditation continues to be a powerful tool for introspection, self-discovery, and overall well-being, transcending its cultural origins to become a global practice.

Benefits of meditation for self-discovery

Meditation is a powerful tool for self-discovery, allowing individuals to embark on an inner journey to explore and understand the depths of their own being. Here are several benefits of meditation for self-discovery:

Heightened Self-Awareness:

Meditation facilitates self-reflection and introspection, enabling individuals to observe their thoughts, emotions, and behaviors objectively. This heightened awareness helps in recognizing patterns and gaining insights into one's own psyche.

Clarity of Mind:

Through regular meditation, the mind becomes clearer and more focused. This mental clarity is essential for self-discovery as it allows individuals to contemplate their values, desires, and purpose with a sharper perspective.

Emotional Regulation:

Meditation teaches individuals to acknowledge and accept their emotions without judgment. By observing emotions during meditation, one can develop the ability to respond to them in a balanced and controlled manner, a crucial skill in self-discovery.

Stress Reduction:

As stress and anxiety levels decrease through meditation, individuals can approach self-reflection and introspection with a calmer mind. This reduced mental noise provides a conducive environment for exploring one's thoughts and feelings more effectively.

Understanding the Ego:

Meditation can offer insights into the nature of the ego and its influence on thoughts, actions, and relationships. By understanding the ego, individuals can begin to differentiate between their true selves and the personas they project.

Connection with Intuition:

Through regular meditation, individuals often report a heightened connection with their intuition or inner wisdom. This intuitive guidance can aid in decision-making, allowing one to align actions with their authentic self.

Discovering Core Values and Beliefs:

Meditation can help individuals identify and clarify their core values, beliefs, and principles. By understanding what truly matters to them, individuals can make life choices that are in harmony with their authentic selves.

Acceptance and Self-Compassion:

Meditation fosters self-compassion and acceptance by promoting a non-judgmental attitude towards oneself. This compassionate approach is fundamental in self-discovery as it allows individuals to accept their imperfections and grow from them.

Deepening the Connection with the Self:

Consistent meditation practice can lead to a profound connection with one's inner self. This deepened connection enables individuals to explore their essence, leading to a greater understanding of their identity beyond societal roles and expectations.

Holistic Well-Being:

Self-discovery through meditation is holistic in nature, impacting mental, emotional, and physical well-being. A balanced and integrated approach to self-exploration can lead to a more fulfilling and purposeful life.

Enhanced Relationships:

Understanding oneself better through meditation can positively impact relationships. When individuals are more in touch with their needs, values, and boundaries, they can cultivate healthier and more authentic connections with others.

Meditation is a transformative pathway to self-discovery, fostering self-awareness, emotional regulation, and a deeper understanding of one's true nature. By exploring the inner landscape of thoughts, emotions, and beliefs, individuals can uncover their authentic selves and lead a more meaningful and fulfilling life.

Meditation Techniques

Meditation encompasses a wide range of techniques, each with its own focus and approach. The choice of course depends on personal preferences, goals, and the desired outcomes. Here are some popular meditation techniques:

Mindfulness Meditation:

Focus: Cultivating awareness of the present moment.

Technique: Paying non-judgmental attention to thoughts, sensations, and emotions as they arise. It often starts with focusing on the breath and gradually expands to all aspects of experience.

Breath Awareness Meditation:

Focus: Observing the breath.

Technique: Concentrating on the natural rhythm of the breath, observing inhalation and exhalation. This practice enhances concentration and helps calm the mind.

Loving-Kindness Meditation (Metta):

Focus: Cultivating feelings of love and compassion.

Technique: Reciting or silently repeating phrases of goodwill and kindness towards oneself and others. It fosters feelings of compassion and empathy.

Body Scan Meditation:

> **Focus**: Scanning the body for tension and relaxation.

> **Technique**: Paying close attention to each part of the body, releasing tension, and promoting physical relaxation. It's often used for stress reduction and relaxation.

Transcendental Meditation (TM):

> **Focus**: A silent mantra or sound.

> **Technique**: Repeating a specific mantra in a specific way to transcend ordinary thought and reach a state of restful awareness. It's a widely practiced form of mantra meditation.

Zen Meditation (Zazen):

> **Focus**: Direct awareness of the present moment.

> **Technique**: Sitting in a specific posture and observing thoughts and sensations as they arise. It often includes focusing on the breath and sometimes contemplating koans (paradoxical statements or questions).

Vipassana Meditation:

> **Focus**: Insight into the true nature of reality.

> **Technique**: Observing the sensations in the body with deep concentration. It's often practiced in silence during intensive retreats.

Chakra Meditation:

> **Focus**: Energy centers in the body (chakras).

Technique: Concentrating on specific chakras to balance and activate energy flow. It's common in various forms of yoga and Hindu and New Age spiritual practices.

Guided Visualization:

Focus: Creating mental images.

Technique: A guided meditation where a teacher or recording leads the practitioner through a visual journey, often designed to manifest a specific goal or intention.

Walking Meditation:

Focus: Combining meditation with walking.

Technique: Slow, deliberate walking with awareness of each step and the sensations in the body. It's practiced in gardens, parks, or designated paths.

Sound Meditation (Nada Yoga):

Focus: Sound or music.

Technique: Listening to soothing sounds, music, or mantras to induce a meditative state. Bowls, gongs, and singing bowls are commonly used.

Body-Mind Meditation:

Focus: The mind-body connection.

Technique: Combines mindfulness with physical movement, such as yoga or Tai Chi. It emphasizes awareness of the body's movements and sensations.

Christian Meditation:

> **Focus**: Spiritual reflection.

> **Technique**: Contemplative prayer or repetition of a sacred word or phrase (e.g., the Jesus Prayer) to deepen one's relationship with God.

Each meditation technique offers unique benefits, and individuals often find the one that resonates most with their goals and preferences. Exploring different techniques and finding what works best for you can be a rewarding journey toward inner peace, self-discovery, and personal growth.

Mindfulness Meditation:

Technique: Mindfulness meditation is a practice that emphasizes non-judgmental awareness of the present moment. Its technique is relatively simple but can be profoundly transformative. Here's how it's typically done:

> **Settle In:** Find a quiet and comfortable place to sit. You can also practice mindfulness while walking, but sitting is a common starting point.

> **Posture:** Sit with your back straight but not rigid. You can sit on a cushion or chair. Rest your hands on your lap or knees. Close your eyes if you prefer or keep them open with a soft gaze on the floor.

> **Focus on Breath:** Bring your attention to your breath. Notice the sensation of the breath as it enters and leaves your nostrils or the rise and fall of your chest or abdomen.

> **Observe Thoughts:** Thoughts will inevitably arise. When they do, don't judge or analyze them. Instead, acknowledge the thought and gently return your focus to the breath.

> **Body Scan:** After a few minutes, you can choose to expand your awareness to your body. Slowly scan from head to toe,

noting any sensations or areas of tension without trying to change them.

Sounds and Environment: Be aware of any sounds around you without attachment or aversion. Also, note any sensations, emotions, or thoughts that arise during the practice.

Non-Judgmental Observation: The key is to observe everything with an open, non-judgmental attitude. Accept the present moment as it is without trying to change it.

Setup: You can practice mindfulness meditation almost anywhere, but setting up a conducive environment can enhance the experience. Here are some considerations:

Location: Choose a quiet place where you won't be easily disturbed.

Seating: Sit comfortably, either on a cushion, chair, or even on the floor if it's comfortable for you.

Timing: Start with a manageable duration, such as 5-10 minutes, and gradually extend it as you become more comfortable.

Distractions: Turn off your phone or put it on silent mode to minimize interruptions.

Lighting: Soft, natural light is ideal, but you can adjust to your preference.

Temperature: Ensure the room is comfortable to avoid distractions.

Attire: Wear loose and comfortable clothing.

Importance: Mindfulness meditation holds significant importance for several reasons:

Stress Reduction: Mindfulness is renowned for its stress-reducing benefits. By focusing on the present moment, it helps individuals disengage from anxious or stressful thoughts about the past or future.

Emotional Regulation: It promotes emotional awareness, allowing individuals to observe their emotions without immediate reaction. This can lead to better emotional regulation and resilience.

Improved Concentration: Mindfulness enhances attention and concentration. This benefit extends to daily tasks and activities, leading to increased productivity and effectiveness.

Enhanced Self-Awareness: Through regular practice, mindfulness fosters a deep understanding of oneself, including thought patterns, habits, and reactions. This self-awareness is vital for personal growth and self-discovery.

Increased Empathy and Compassion: Mindfulness often leads to greater empathy and compassion, as it encourages an open-hearted, non-judgmental attitude toward oneself and others.

Better Decision-Making: By cultivating awareness and reducing impulsivity, mindfulness can lead to more considered and thoughtful decision-making.

Focus: Mindfulness meditation focuses primarily on:

Breath: The sensation of the breath serves as an anchor to the present moment. It is a continuous and readily accessible point of focus.

Body Sensations: The practice often involves scanning the body to observe physical sensations, such as tension or relaxation.

Thoughts and Emotions: Mindfulness encourages the non-judgmental observation of thoughts and emotions as they arise. This helps individuals detach from their thoughts and see them as passing phenomena rather than absolute truths.

The Present Moment: The core focus is always on the here and now, cultivating an attentive presence to whatever is happening at the moment.

In essence, mindfulness meditation is about being fully present in each moment, cultivating a deep awareness of your inner and outer experiences, and embracing life with greater clarity, acceptance, and equanimity.

Breath Awareness Meditation:

Technique: Breath awareness meditation, also known as breath meditation or mindful breathing, is a foundational meditation practice that centers on the breath as the primary object of focus. Here's a detailed description of the technique:

Setup:

Posture: Find a comfortable seated position. You can sit on a cushion or a chair with your back straight but not rigid. Alternatively, you can practice lying down, but sitting is often recommended to avoid falling asleep.

Eyes: Close your eyes gently, or keep them open with a soft gaze, depending on your preference.

Hands: Rest your hands on your lap, with your palms facing up or down, whichever feels more comfortable.

Focus on the Breath:

Direct your attention to your breath. Pay close attention to the natural rhythm of your breath without trying to control it.

You can focus on the sensation of the breath at a specific point, such as the nostrils (feeling the coolness of the inhale and warmth of the exhale) or the rising and falling of your abdomen or chest.

Observe the Breath:

As you focus on your breath, become a passive observer. Observe each inhalation and exhalation as they come and go.

Notice the entire breath cycle, from the moment the breath enters your body to the moment it leaves.

Mind-Wandering and Distractions:

Your mind will inevitably wander, and distractions will arise. When this happens, gently acknowledge the distraction without judgment, and then return your attention to the breath.

It's normal for the mind to wander repeatedly during meditation. Each time you notice it, consider it an opportunity to practice coming back to the breath.

Duration:

Start with a manageable duration, such as 5-10 minutes, and gradually extend it as you become more comfortable with the practice.

You can use a timer to signal the end of your meditation session.

Importance: Breath awareness meditation holds significant importance for several reasons:

Calms the Mind: Focusing on the breath helps quiet the mental chatter and promotes relaxation, reducing stress and anxiety.

Enhances Concentration: It improves concentration and attention span, benefiting daily tasks and productivity.

Cultivates Presence: Breath awareness encourages living in the present moment, reducing rumination about the past or worrying about the future.

Emotional Regulation: By observing the breath, individuals can better manage their emotional responses and cultivate emotional resilience.

Physical Benefits: It can lead to improved respiratory function, lower blood pressure, and overall well-being.

Gateway to Deeper Meditation: Breath awareness is often used as a foundational practice in more advanced meditation techniques.

Focus: Breath awareness meditation primarily focuses on the following aspects:

Sensation of Breath: The physical sensations associated with breathing, such as the feeling of the breath entering and leaving the body, the rise and fall of the abdomen or chest, and the quality of the breath (shallow, deep, smooth, irregular).

Mindfulness of the Present Moment: The practice emphasizes cultivating a mindful presence in the here and now, anchored by the continuous and rhythmic nature of the breath.

Observation of the Mind: It also involves observing the nature of the mind itself, including how it tends to wander and how it responds to distractions.

Breath awareness meditation is not only a valuable standalone practice but also a foundational skill that can be incorporated into various meditation traditions and daily life to cultivate greater mindfulness, focus, and inner calm.

Loving-Kindness Meditation (Metta):

Technique: Loving-Kindness Meditation, often referred to as Metta (which means "loving-kindness" in Pali, an ancient Indian language), is a meditation practice rooted in cultivating feelings of love, compassion, and goodwill toward oneself and others. Here's how to practice Metta meditation:

> **Posture:** Find a comfortable seated position on a cushion or a chair. Maintain an upright but relaxed posture.
>
> **Eyes:** Close your eyes gently.
>
> **Hands:** Place your hands on your lap, with your palms facing up or down, or you can place your right hand over your heart as a gesture of self-compassion.

Begin with Self-Compassion:

> Start by directing loving-kindness towards yourself. In your mind, silently repeat phrases like "May I be happy," "May I be healthy," "May I be safe," and "May I live with ease."
>
> Feel the warmth and sincerity of these phrases. You can customize them to suit your needs or use traditional Metta phrases.

Expand Loving-Kindness:

> Gradually extend your loving-kindness to others, starting with loved ones, friends, acquaintances, and eventually to all beings, including those you

may have conflicts with or hold negative feelings towards.

For each group, silently repeat similar phrases, such as "May [name] be happy," "May [name] be healthy," etc. Visualize their happiness and well-being.

Maintain a Loving Heart:

Continue to radiate loving-kindness to all beings, without discrimination. Feel a genuine sense of love and compassion in your heart as you do this.

If your mind wanders or negative emotions arise, gently return your focus to the practice and the phrases.

Closure:

After a suitable period, bring your awareness back to yourself and end the practice with another round of Metta for yourself.

Take a few deep breaths, slowly open your eyes, and carry the feelings of loving-kindness with you into your day.

Importance: Loving-Kindness Meditation (Metta) holds several important benefits:

Cultivates Compassion: Metta meditation nurtures compassion and kindness, fostering a more compassionate attitude toward oneself and others.

Promotes Emotional Healing: It can be particularly beneficial for individuals struggling with self-criticism, low self-esteem, or unresolved emotional wounds. Metta helps heal emotional scars.

Reduces Negative Emotions: Metta counteracts negative emotions like anger, resentment, and jealousy by replacing them with positive feelings of love and goodwill.

Enhances Relationships: Practicing Metta improves one's ability to relate to others with empathy, forgiveness, and understanding, which can lead to healthier and more harmonious relationships.

Increases Self-Love: It encourages self-love and self-acceptance, fostering a sense of worthiness and well-being.

Cultivates Joy: As Metta generates feelings of love and goodwill, it often leads to an increased sense of joy and happiness.

Focus: Loving-Kindness Meditation (Metta) focuses on:

Feelings of Love and Compassion: The primary focus is on generating and cultivating feelings of love, kindness, and compassion within oneself and extending them to others.

Phrases of Loving-Kindness: The practice often uses specific phrases or affirmations to channel loving-kindness. These phrases express positive intentions for happiness, health, safety, and ease for oneself and others.

Visualization: Practitioners may visualize the individuals they are directing Metta towards, imagining their happiness, well-being, and inner peace.

Metta meditation is not only a powerful tool for personal transformation but also a way to contribute to a more compassionate and connected world by radiating love and goodwill to all beings, regardless of differences or conflicts.

Body Scan Meditation:

Technique: Body Scan Meditation is a mindfulness practice that involves directing focused attention to various parts of the body systematically. This technique promotes awareness of physical sensations, relaxation, and a deeper connection between the mind and body. Here's how to practice Body Scan Meditation:

Posture: Find a comfortable seated or lying-down position. If sitting, ensure that your back is straight but not rigid. If lying down, use a yoga mat or soft surface.

Eyes: Close your eyes gently.

Hands: Rest your hands on your lap (if sitting) or at your sides (if lying down).

Beginning with Breath:

Start by taking a few deep breaths to center yourself. Inhale deeply through your nose and exhale slowly through your mouth.

Bring your awareness to your breath, feeling the rise and fall of your chest or the sensation of your breath entering and leaving your nostrils. Spend a few moments focusing on your breath to settle into the present moment.

Systematic Scanning:

Begin at the top of your head and slowly move your attention down your body. Please pay close attention to each part of your body as you mentally scan through it.

As you focus on each area, observe any physical sensations without judgment. Notice any tension, discomfort, warmth, coolness, or relaxation that you may feel.

Progression:

Continue to move your attention methodically down your body, through areas like the forehead, eyes, nose, mouth, neck, shoulders, chest, arms, abdomen, pelvis, legs, and feet.

Spend a few moments on each part, breathing naturally and allowing any tension or discomfort to melt away through your mindful attention.

Awareness and Relaxation:

Body Scan Meditation is an opportunity to release physical tension and promote relaxation. As you become more aware of areas of tension, consciously relax those areas.

If you encounter areas of tension or discomfort, breathe into them and imagine the tension dissipating with each exhalation.

Closing and Reawakening:

When you have scanned your entire body, take a few moments to experience your body as a whole. Feel the sensation of your entire body at rest.

Slowly bring your awareness back to your breath. Take a few deep breaths to reawaken your body and mind.

Importance: Body Scan Meditation offers several important benefits:

Stress Reduction: By systematically relaxing the body and releasing tension, Body Scan Meditation can significantly reduce stress and anxiety.

Mind-Body Connection: It enhances the connection between the mind and body, fostering a greater awareness of how mental states and emotions manifest physically.

Physical Relaxation: The practice promotes physical relaxation, which can lead to improved sleep, reduced muscle tension, and a greater sense of well-being.

Pain Management: Body Scan Meditation is often used as a complementary technique for managing chronic pain by increasing awareness of and reducing the perception of pain.

Mindfulness Training: It's an effective way to cultivate mindfulness, as it encourages non-judgmental observation of physical sensations and feelings in the body.

Focus: Body Scan Meditation primarily focuses on:

Physical Sensations: The practice emphasizes observing and experiencing physical sensations in various parts of the body.

Tension and Relaxation: It encourages awareness of areas of tension and facilitates relaxation in those areas through focused attention and breath.

Mind-Body Connection: Body Scan Meditation enhances the connection between the mind and body, making practitioners more attuned to how thoughts and emotions manifest physically.

Overall, Body Scan Meditation is a valuable practice for promoting relaxation, reducing stress, and deepening mindfulness by cultivating a heightened awareness of the body and its sensations.

Transcendental Meditation (TM):

Technique: Transcendental Meditation (TM) is a specific form of mantra meditation that focuses on achieving a unique state of restful awareness. The technique is straightforward and involves the following steps:

Posture: Find a comfortable seated position with your back straight, but not rigid, and your hands resting on your lap.

Eyes: Close your eyes gently.

Selection of Mantra:

TM practitioners are given a specific mantra by a certified TM instructor. The mantra is a meaningless word or sound chosen for its vibrational qualities.

The mantra is to be kept secret and should not be shared with others.

Repetition of Mantra:

Begin silently repeating the mantra in your mind. It is repeated effortlessly and without force.

You repeat the mantra in a rhythmic manner, allowing it to flow naturally, like a mental vibration or sound.

Thoughts and Awareness:

As you continue to repeat the mantra, you may notice other thoughts and distractions arising. This is natural.

When you become aware of these thoughts or distractions, gently and without effort, return your attention to the repetition of the mantra.

Duration:

TM sessions typically last for about 15-20 minutes, but it can be practiced for longer periods if desired.

It is recommended to practice TM twice daily, ideally once in the morning and once in the evening.

Ending the Practice:

After the allotted time, stop repeating the mantra and sit quietly with your eyes closed for a few moments.

Then, open your eyes, stand up, and continue with your daily activities.

Importance: Transcendental Meditation (TM) has gained recognition and popularity for several reasons:

Stress Reduction: TM is known for its effectiveness in reducing stress and anxiety. It induces a state of deep relaxation, allowing the body to recover from the effects of stress.

Improved Focus and Clarity: The practice enhances concentration and mental clarity, which can improve decision-making and cognitive functioning.

Enhanced Creativity: TM practitioners often report increased creativity and problem-solving abilities.

Emotional Well-Being: TM can help manage and reduce symptoms of anxiety and depression, promoting emotional balance.

Better Sleep: Regular TM practice can improve the quality of sleep, making it easier to fall asleep and stay asleep.

Increased Self-Awareness: TM can foster a deeper sense of self-awareness and personal growth.

Focus: Transcendental Meditation (TM) primarily focuses on:

Mantra Repetition: The core focus is on the effortless repetition of the assigned mantra. The mantra serves as a vehicle to help transcend ordinary thought and reach a state of restful awareness.

Restful Awareness: TM aims to lead practitioners to a state of deep restful awareness where thought activity becomes less dominant, and a sense of inner calm and stillness is experienced.

Effortless Meditation: Unlike other forms of meditation that may involve concentration or visualization, TM emphasizes effortlessness, allowing thoughts to come and go naturally.

Inner Experience: The practice is focused on inner experience and is less concerned with external stimuli or the monitoring of bodily sensations.

It's important to note that TM is typically taught by certified instructors through a personalized process, including individual instruction and follow-up sessions. The specific mantra assigned to each practitioner is chosen based on their individual characteristics and needs. This individualized approach is a hallmark of TM instruction.

Zen Meditation (Zazen):

Technique: Zen Meditation, often referred to as Zazen, is a foundational practice in Zen Buddhism. It emphasizes seated meditation to develop mindfulness, concentration, and insight. Here's how to practice Zazen:

Posture: Find a comfortable and stable seated position. The traditional posture is the full lotus or half-lotus position, but many practitioners use a chair or cushion (zafu) to sit cross-legged.

Back: Keep your back straight but not stiff. It should be naturally aligned, forming a gentle curve in your lower back.

Hands: Place your hands in the cosmic mudra: left hand resting on the right hand, palms up, with the thumbs lightly touching and forming an oval shape. The hands should rest on your lap, close to your body.

Eyes: Keep your eyes open, with your gaze directed downward.. Maintain a soft focus a few feet in front of you.

Breathing:

Breathe naturally through your nose. Pay attention to your breath without attempting to control it.

Focus on the sensation of the breath as it enters and leaves your nostrils or the rise and fall of your abdomen with each breath.

Mindfulness and Concentration:

Bring your attention to the present moment. Be aware of your posture, the sensations in your body, and the sound of your breath.

When thoughts arise, acknowledge them without judgment and gently return your attention to your breath and posture.

Timing:

Zazen sessions can vary in length but often last between 20-40 minutes.

You can use a timer to signal the end of your session.

Silence:

> is practiced in silence. There is no need for verbal chants, mantras, or guided instructions Zazen during the session.

Importance: Zazen is a fundamental practice in Zen Buddhism, and it holds several important benefits:

> **Mindfulness and Presence:** Zazen cultivates mindfulness and a deep sense of presence in the here and now. It encourages practitioners to be fully aware of each moment as it unfolds.

> **Clarity of Mind:** The practice sharpens concentration and mental clarity, which can enhance one's ability to see things as they are and to respond to life's challenges with wisdom.

> **Insight and Self-Discovery:** Through sustained meditation, practitioners often experience insights into the nature of the self and reality. These insights can lead to profound personal transformation.

> **Emotional Balance:** Zazen can help individuals develop emotional resilience and equanimity. It encourages a non-reactive awareness of emotions as they arise.

> **Inner Peace:** Regular practice can lead to a profound sense of inner peace and contentment.

Focus: Zen Meditation (Zazen) primarily focuses on:

> **Breath:** The breath serves as an anchor for mindfulness. Practitioners pay close attention to the natural rhythm of their breath, using it as a focal point to maintain awareness.

> **Posture:** Correct posture is essential in Zazen. The body's position reflects the mind's state, and maintaining an upright, balanced posture is considered crucial for mental clarity and insight.

Observation of Thoughts: When thoughts arise, practitioners are encouraged to observe them without attachment or aversion. Zazen aims to develop the ability to watch thoughts come and go without getting entangled in them.

Present-Moment Awareness: The core focus of Zazen is on being fully present in each moment. It encourages a direct and unmediated experience of reality as it is, free from conceptualization and interpretation.

In summary, Zazen is a profound meditation practice that fosters mindfulness, concentration, and insight. It emphasizes simplicity, silence, and the direct experience of the present moment. Through dedicated practice, individuals can deepen their understanding of themselves and the nature of reality, leading to personal growth and spiritual awakening.

Vipassana Meditation:

Technique: Vipassana Meditation is a traditional Buddhist meditation practice that aims to develop insight and wisdom by observing the true nature of reality. It involves systematic mindfulness and awareness of one's bodily sensations, thoughts, and emotions. Here's how to practice Vipassana:

Posture: Find a comfortable seated position on a cushion or chair. Keep your back straight but not rigid. You can also practice while lying down if necessary.

Eyes: Close your eyes gently.

Hands: Place your hands on your lap or knees, with your palms facing up or down, whichever feels more comfortable.

Breath Awareness:

Start by focusing on your breath for a few moments. Pay attention to the natural rhythm of your breath, using it to anchor your awareness to the present moment.

Body Scanning:

Begin systematically scanning your body from head to toe or toe to head, noting any sensations you encounter.

Pay close attention to physical sensations, such as pressure, warmth, tingling, tension, or discomfort.

Observe sensations objectively, without attachment or aversion. If you notice discomfort, explore it with curiosity rather than trying to escape it.

Thoughts and Emotions:

As thoughts and emotions arise during the practice, acknowledge them without judgment. Let them come and go like passing clouds.

Refocus your attention on the bodily sensations when your mind wanders.

Mindful Walking:

Vipassana can also be practiced while walking. Slowly and mindfully walk in a designated area, paying attention to each step and the sensations in your feet and legs.

Duration:

> Vipassana sessions can vary in length, but they often last from 20-60 minutes or longer, depending on your experience and comfort level.

Closure:

> To end the practice, slowly bring your awareness back to your breath (if you started with breath awareness) or to your physical posture.
>
> Take a few deep breaths, gently open your eyes, and return to your regular activities.

Importance: Vipassana Meditation is highly regarded for its transformative effects and has several important benefits:

> **Insight and Wisdom:** Vipassana aims to deepen one's understanding of the true nature of reality, leading to profound insights and wisdom.
>
> **Emotional Regulation:** By observing thoughts and emotions without attachment, Vipassana helps practitioners develop emotional resilience and balance.
>
> **Stress Reduction:** The practice promotes relaxation and stress reduction by anchoring one's attention to the present moment.
>
> **Enhanced Concentration:** Vipassana sharpens concentration and mental clarity, which can improve daily tasks and decision-making.
>
> **Self-Discovery:** Through mindful observation, individuals can gain a deeper understanding of themselves, including their habitual thought patterns and reactions.

Focus: Vipassana Meditation primarily focuses on:

> **Bodily Sensations:** The core of Vipassana is the observation of physical sensations throughout the body. These sensations are considered a gateway to understanding the impermanence and interconnectedness of all experiences.

> **Thoughts and Emotions:** While bodily sensations are the primary focus, thoughts and emotions are also observed as they arise. The key is to observe them with equanimity, recognizing their transient nature.

> **Present-Moment Awareness:** Vipassana emphasizes being fully present in the here and now. It encourages direct and unmediated awareness of reality as it unfolds, free from concepts and interpretations.

In Vipassana, the process of observation is characterized by mindfulness, objectivity, and non-attachment. By cultivating these qualities and exploring the impermanence of all phenomena, practitioners aim to achieve greater clarity, insight, and a deepened understanding of the nature of suffering and liberation, as taught in Buddhist philosophy

Chakra Meditation:

Technique: Chakra meditation is a practice rooted in various spiritual and healing traditions, particularly within Hinduism and the New Age movement. It focuses on the body's energy centers, known as chakras, to promote balance, healing, and spiritual growth. Here's how to practice Chakra Meditation:

> **Posture:** Find a comfortable seated or lying-down position. You can use a cushion, chair, or yoga mat.

> **Eyes:** Close your eyes gently.

> **Hands:** Rest your hands on your lap, with your palms facing up or down, or position your hands over each chakra point.

Relaxation and Centering:

Begin with a few deep breaths to relax and center yourself.

Focus on your intention for the meditation, whether it's to balance your chakras, promote healing, or connect with higher consciousness.

Chakra Focus:

Start at the root chakra, which is located at the base of the spine. Visualize or imagine a spinning, vibrant red wheel of energy at this point.

Move up through each chakra, one by one, focusing on their corresponding colors and positions:

Sacral Chakra (Orange) - Below the navel

Solar Plexus Chakra (Yellow) - Upper abdomen

Heart Chakra (Green or Pink) - Center of the chest

Throat Chakra (Blue) - Throat

Third Eye Chakra (Indigo) - Between the eyebrows

Crown Chakra (Violet or White) - Top of the head

Spend a few minutes on each chakra, imagining them as spinning wheels or vibrant orbs of light. Visualize them becoming balanced, clear, and aligned.

Breathing and Affirmations:

As you focus on each chakra, take deep, mindful breaths. Inhale positive energy, and exhale any blockages or negativity associated with the chakra.

You can also use affirmations or mantras specific to each chakra to enhance the meditation.

Healing and Releasing:

If you sense blockages or unresolved emotions associated with a particular chakra, use this meditation as an opportunity to release and heal them.

Imagine any negative energy or emotions being transformed into positive energy and flowing freely through the chakra.

Completion:

After you have focused on all the chakras, take a few moments to experience the alignment and balance of your energy centers.

Slowly bring your awareness back to your breath and physical body.

When you feel ready, gently open your eyes and transition back to your daily activities.

Importance: Chakra meditation holds several potential benefits:

Balancing Energy: The practice aims to balance the flow of energy through the chakras, promoting physical, emotional, and spiritual well-being.

Healing: Chakra meditation can be used to address emotional wounds, traumas, or unresolved issues that may be stored in the energy centers.

Enhancing Awareness: By focusing on the chakras, individuals can develop a deeper understanding of their own energy patterns and emotional states.

Spiritual Growth: Chakra meditation is often usedfor spiritual development, aiming to open the chakras to higher consciousness and wisdom.

Emotional Regulation: It can help individuals manage and regulate their emotions by addressing imbalances in the energy centers.

Focus: Chakra meditation primarily focuses on:

Chakra Visualization: The core of this meditation is visualizing or sensing the chakras as spinning wheels or orbs of light, each with its corresponding color.

Energy Flow: The practice involves promoting the healthy and balanced flow of energy through each chakra, ensuring that they are clear, open, and functioning optimally.

Affirmations or Mantras: Specific affirmations or mantras may be used to address the qualities and issues associated with each chakra, such as self-confidence, love, or communication.

Healing and Transformation: Chakra meditation often transforms negative energy or emotions into positive, healing energy. This can be a significant focus, especially if you are working through emotional blockages or traumas.

Chakra meditation is a holistic approach to well-being that integrates the mind, body, and spirit. It is used for personal growth, healing, and self-discovery, and it can be tailored to meet individual needs and intentions

Guided Visualization:

Technique: Guided visualization is a form of meditation that involves mentally creating and exploring vivid, detailed scenarios or images guided by an external source, such as a meditation teacher or recorded audio. It's designed to engage your senses and imagination to achieve various goals, such as relaxation, personal growth, or problem-solving. Here's how to practice guided visualization:

Setup:

Environment: Find a quiet, comfortable space where you won't be disturbed. It can be seated in a chair, lying down, or in any posture that allows you to relax.

Audio: Prepare a guided visualization recording or find one online. You can also have a meditation teacher or practitioner guide you in person.

Relaxation:

Close your eyes and take a few deep breaths to relax your body and mind.

Allow your body to settle into a comfortable position, releasing any tension.

Guidance:

Listen to the guided visualization. The narrator or guide will provide instructions and descriptions to help you create a mental image of the scenario or journey.

Follow their cues as they lead you through the visualization.

Imagination and Senses:

Engage your imagination and senses. Visualize the details of the scenario—colors, shapes, textures, sounds, smells, and tastes.

Immerse yourself in the experience, making it as vivid and real as possible.

Emotional Engagement:

Pay attention to the emotions and feelings that arise during the visualization. Allow yourself to experience and embrace these emotions fully.

Completion:

When the guided visualization ends, slowly bring your awareness back to your physical surroundings.

Take a few deep breaths and open your eyes.

Reflect on your experience and any insights or feelings that arose during the practice.

Importance: Guided visualization is a versatile and valuable practice with several key benefits:

Stress Reduction: It promotes relaxation and reduces stress by redirecting your focus away from worries and anxieties, creating a calming mental space.

Enhanced Creativity: Visualization exercises can stimulate your creative thinking and problem-solving abilities by allowing you to explore new perspectives and solutions.

Goal Achievement: Guided visualization can be used to help clarify and manifest your goals by mentally rehearsing and visualizing the steps and outcomes.

Emotional Healing: It can be a powerful tool for processing and healing emotional wounds, as it allows you to engage with and release emotions in a controlled and supportive environment.

Improved Focus: Guided visualization enhances concentration and can improve your ability to concentrate on specific tasks or objectives.

Personal Growth: Many guided visualizations are designed to support personal growth and self-discovery by exploring various aspects of yourself and your life.

Focus: Guided visualization can focus on a wide range of scenarios and objectives, depending on the specific meditation or goal. Some common areas of focus include:

Relaxation: Guided visualizations for relaxation often take you on a peaceful mental journey to a tranquil location, helping you unwind and reduce stress.

Healing: Visualizations for healing may involve visualizing the body's natural healing processes or imagining the release of emotional or physical pain.

Goal Achievement: These visualizations are geared toward helping you achieve specific goals, such as career success, weight loss, or personal development.

Self-Discovery: Guided visualizations can help you explore your inner world, discover your passions, or gain insights into your life's purpose.

Empowerment: Some visualizations focus on enhancing your self-esteem, confidence, or self-worth.

Problem-Solving: Visualization can be a creative tool for brainstorming solutions to challenges or dilemmas.

The power of guided visualization lies in its ability to harness the imagination and the mind's capacity to create and transform mental images. When done regularly and with intention, guided visualization can be a valuable tool for personal growth and well-being.

Walking Meditation:

Technique: Walking meditation is a form of mindfulness practice that involves walking slowly and deliberately, paying full attention to the act of walking and the sensations associated with it. It can be a valuable complement to seated meditation and offers an opportunity to cultivate mindfulness in motion. Here's how to practice walking meditation:

> **Environment:** Choose a quiet, safe place to walk. This can be indoors or outdoors. It's essential that the environment is conducive to mindfulness, free from distractions.
>
> **Posture:** Stand still for a moment to establish a comfortable, upright posture. Your feet should be parallel, with your weight evenly distributed.

Intention and Mindset:

> Set a clear intention for your walking meditation practice. It might be to cultivate mindfulness, relieve stress, or enjoy the experience of walking.
>
> Approach the practice with an open, non-judgmental mindset. Be fully present in each moment.

Walking Steps:

> Begin to walk at a very slow and deliberate pace. Lift one foot, move it forward, and place it down with full awareness.
>
> Coordinate your breath with your steps if it feels natural. For example, you might take one step with each inhalation and one step with each exhalation.

Pay close attention to the physical sensations associated with walking: the lifting, moving, and placing of each foot.

Focus on Sensations:

Direct your attention to the sensations in your feet and legs as they make contact with the ground. Notice the pressure, temperature, and texture of the surface beneath you.

Observe any subtle movements in your body as you walk. Maintain an upright posture with a straight back and relaxed shoulders.

Mindful Presence:

As your mind inevitably wanders, gently guide your attention back to the physical sensations of walking.

Be aware of any thoughts, emotions, or distractions that arise, and let them come and go without judgment.

Turning Around:

If you have enough space, you can continue walking in a straight line. If not, choose a designated spot to stop and turn around mindfully.

When turning, pause for a moment to bring your awareness to your intentions and the transition.

Returning to Walking:

Resume walking in the opposite direction, maintaining the same level of mindfulness and attention to each step.

Completion:

> When you decide to conclude your walking meditation session, stand still for a moment and take a few deep breaths.
>
> Transition back to regular walking or your next activity with awareness, carrying the mindfulness cultivated during the practice with you.

Importance: Walking meditation offers several important benefits:

Mindfulness in Motion: It allows you to practice mindfulness and presence while engaging in a common daily activity, which can be particularly helpful for those who struggle with seated meditation.

Stress Reduction: Walking meditation can promote relaxation and reduce stress by redirecting your focus away from worries and anxieties.

Improved Concentration: The practice enhances concentration and can improve your ability to stay focused on tasks in your daily life.

Physical Awareness: It encourages a deeper connection to your body, promoting better posture, balance, and physical awareness.

Emotional Regulation: Walking meditation can help you manage emotions and cultivate emotional resilience by addressing them mindfully as they arise.

Focus: Walking meditation primarily focuses on:

Walking Steps: The core of this practice is the act of walking itself. Attention is directed to the lifting, moving, and placing of each foot with full awareness.

Sensations: The primary focus is on physical sensations in the feet, legs, and body as they make contact with the ground and engage in the walking process.

Breath Coordination (Optional): Some practitioners coordinate their breath with their steps, taking one step with each inhalation and exhalation. This can enhance mindfulness and rhythm.

Present-Moment Awareness: Walking meditation emphasizes being fully present in each step and moment, allowing distractions and thoughts to come and go without attachment.

Overall, walking meditation is a valuable practice for grounding yourself in the present moment, cultivating mindfulness in everyday activities, and finding peace and stillness within motion. It can be adapted to various settings and is accessible to individuals of all fitness levels.

Sound Meditation (Nada Yoga):

Technique: Sound meditation, often referred to as Nada Yoga in the yogic tradition, is a practice that uses sound as a focal point to cultivate mindfulness, inner stillness, and spiritual awareness. It involves listening to and meditating on various sounds, including external sounds and internal sounds produced within the body, such as the sound of one's breath or inner vibrations. Here's how to practice sound meditation:

Environment: Find a quiet and peaceful space where you can sit comfortably without distractions.

Posture: Sit in a comfortable meditation posture with your back straight and your hands resting on your lap. You can also practice sound meditation while lying down if preferred.

Eyes: Close your eyes gently to minimize external visual distractions.

External Sounds:

Begin by listening to the sounds around you without judgment or attachment. Pay attention to the subtlest of sounds, such as the rustling of leaves, birdsong, or distant traffic.

Instead of categorizing sounds as pleasant or unpleasant, practice impartial listening, observing each sound as it arises and passes away.

Internal Sounds:

Shift your attention to the sounds produced within your body. Focus on the rhythm of your breath, the sound of your heartbeat, or any other internal vibrations or sensations.

If you find it challenging to perceive internal sounds, place your attention on the breath as it moves in and out. Listen to the sound of your own inhalation and exhalation.

Mantra or Sacred Sounds (Optional):

You may choose to introduce a mantra, chant, or sacred sound into your practice. These can be repeated silently or audibly and serve as a focal point for meditation.

Traditional mantras like "Om" or "Aum" are commonly used in Nada Yoga.

Deep Listening:

Engage in deep listening, which means paying full attention to the subtleties and nuances of sound.

As you listen, let go of any mental chatter or analysis and allow the act of listening to become your sole focus.

Inner Stillness:

> With continued practice, you may begin to experience a sense of inner stillness and peace that arises from your attentive listening.

> This inner silence can lead to heightened awareness and deep states of meditation.

Completion:

> When you decide to conclude your sound meditation session, slowly bring your awareness back to your surroundings.

> Open your eyes gently, stretch, and transition back to your daily activities with mindfulness.

Importance: Sound meditation (Nada Yoga) carries several important benefits:

Mindfulness and Presence: It cultivates mindfulness by encouraging focused attention on sounds, whether external or internal, and promotes a deep sense of presence.

Inner Stillness: Sound meditation can lead to inner silence and stillness, helping to calm the mind and reduce mental chatter.

Emotional Regulation: The practice can aid in emotional regulation by providing a non-reactive space to observe emotions as they arise in response to sounds.

Spiritual Exploration: Nada Yoga is considered a path to spiritual awakening, as it can lead to profound insights and experiences related to the nature of consciousness and the self.

Enhanced Listening Skills: Regular practice of sound meditation can improve your listening skills, making you more attuned to the subtleties of sound in everyday life.

Focus: Sound meditation, or Nada Yoga, primarily focuses on:

Listening: The core of this practice is attentive listening to various sounds, both external and internal, without judgment or attachment.

Deep Listening: The emphasis is on deep listening, which involves paying full and undivided attention to the intricacies and subtleties of sound.

Inner Stillness: As you engage in sound meditation, the ultimate focus is to discover inner stillness and silence that underlies all sound.

Mantras and Sacred Sounds: Some practitioners incorporate mantras or sacred sounds into their practice as a way to deepen their meditation and connect with spiritual aspects of sound.

Overall, sound meditation (Nada Yoga) is a practice that harnesses the power of sound to deepen mindfulness, explore consciousness, and foster inner peace and awareness. It is a versatile form of meditation that can be adapted to various settings and customized to individual preferences and spiritual beliefs.

Body-Mind Meditation:

Technique: Body-mind meditation is a holistic practice that combines mindfulness of the body with mental awareness to cultivate a deep sense of presence and self-awareness. It involves paying close attention to bodily sensations, movements, and postures while also observing thoughts, emotions, and the mind's activities. Here's how to practice body-mind meditation:

Environment: Find a quiet and comfortable space for your practice where you won't be disturbed. It can be practiced seated on a cushion or chair, or you can lie down if preferred.

Posture: Assume a comfortable yet alert posture. Keep your back straight but not rigid, allowing for a natural alignment.

Eyes: Close your eyes gently to minimize visual distractions.

Body Awareness:

Begin by directing your attention to the physical sensations in your body. Start from the top of your head and gradually move your awareness down through your body.

Notice any areas of tension, discomfort, or relaxation. Pay attention to the temperature, pressure, and vibrations in different parts of your body.

Breath Awareness:

Shift your focus to your breath. Observe the natural rhythm of your breath without attempting to control it.

Pay attention to the rise and fall of your chest or the sensation of your breath passing through your nostrils.

Sensations and Movements:

As you continue to breathe mindfully, be aware of any sensations or movements in your body. This might include the expansion and contraction of your abdomen with each breath or the feeling of your body resting on the floor or chair.

If you notice any discomfort or tension, explore it with curiosity and allow it to be without judgment.

Thoughts and Emotions:

While maintaining awareness of your body and breath, observe your thoughts and emotions as they arise. Notice the content of your thoughts and the emotions associated with them.

Avoid getting caught up in the stories or judgments associated with your thoughts. Instead, view them as passing mental phenomena.

Integration:

Bring your attention back to your body and breath, integrating the awareness of your physical sensations, breath, thoughts, and emotions.

Allow your body and mind to coexist in the present moment without prioritizing one over the other.

Completion:

When you decide to conclude your body-mind meditation, slowly bring your awareness back to your surroundings.

Open your eyes gently, stretch, and transition back to your daily activities with mindfulness.

Importance: Body-mind meditation offers several important benefits:

Mind-Body Connection: It deepens the connection between the mind and body, fostering greater awareness of how mental states influence physical sensations and vice versa.

Stress Reduction: By observing bodily tension and mental states, body-mind meditation can help reduce stress and promote relaxation.

Emotional Regulation: The practice enhances emotional regulation by allowing you to observe emotions as bodily sensations and mental activities.

Self-Awareness: Body-mind meditation promotes self-awareness and self-acceptance by encouraging non-judgmental observation of your inner experience.

Mindfulness and Presence: It cultivates mindfulness and presence by focusing on both the body and the mind in the present moment.

Enhanced Focus: Regular practice can improve concentration and mental clarity, enhancing your ability to stay focused in everyday life.

Focus: Body-mind meditation primarily focuses on:

Body Awareness: The core of this practice is paying attention to bodily sensations, movements, and postures with a sense of curiosity and non-judgment.

Breath Awareness: The breath serves as an anchor for mindfulness. Observing the breath helps maintain present-moment awareness and a connection between the body and mind.

Thoughts and Emotions: While focusing on the body and breath, you also observe thoughts and emotions as they arise, without getting entangled in them or attempting to suppress them.

Integration: The practice aims to integrate body and mind, emphasizing that they are interconnected aspects of your present experience.

Body-mind meditation is a holistic practice that invites you to explore the intricate relationship between your physical sensations, thoughts, emotions, and breath. Through regular practice, you can develop a deeper understanding of yourself, reduce stress, and cultivate mindfulness and presence in your daily life.

Christian Meditation:

Technique: Christian meditation is a contemplative practice rooted in Christian spirituality and aimed at deepening one's relationship with God. It involves prayerful reflection, silence, and stillness to foster a sense of divine presence and communion. Here's how to practice Christian meditation:

Environment: Find a quiet and peaceful place for your practice, free from distractions.

Posture: Sit or kneel in a comfortable yet upright position. Some practitioners prefer to use a straight-backed chair, while others may choose to sit on a cushion.

Eyes: Close your eyes gently or maintain a soft, unfocused gaze.

Centering Prayer:

Begin with a simple prayer or invocation, such as the Lord's Prayer or a phrase from Scripture, to set your intention and invite the presence of God.

Silent Contemplation:

Enter into a state of silence and stillness. Release any distractions or thoughts as they arise, returning your focus to God's presence.

Some practitioners use a sacred word or phrase (known as a mantra or prayer word) as a point of focus. This word is repeated silently in rhythm with the breath to help maintain a contemplative state.

Listening and Openness:

Be open to listening to God's presence rather than actively seeking insights or answers. Allow yourself to be receptive to God's communication in whatever form it may take.

Reflect on Scripture:

Another form of Christian meditation involves reading and reflecting on a passage from the Bible. Choose a short passage or verse and read it slowly, allowing the words to sink in.

Reflect on the meaning of the scripture in the context of your life and your relationship with God.

Contemplation and Presence:

Shift your focus from active thinking to contemplation. In this state, you are not analyzing or interpreting; you are simply being present with God.

Completion:

When you decide to conclude your Christian meditation session, offer a closing prayer of gratitude and blessing. Slowly bring your awareness back to your surroundings.

Importance: Christian meditation serves several significant purposes within Christian spirituality:

Deepening Faith: It is a means of deepening one's faith and connection with God through direct communion and contemplation.

Spiritual Growth: Christian meditation fosters spiritual growth by inviting individuals to explore their inner world and develop a more profound relationship with the divine.

Peace and Serenity: The practice often brings a sense of peace, serenity, and inner stillness, helping individuals find solace in the presence of God.

Reflection on Scripture: Many Christian meditators use this practice to reflect on the teachings and wisdom found in the Bible, seeking to apply these insights to their lives.

Community and Worship: Christian meditation can be practiced individually or in a group setting as a form of communal worship and spiritual support.

Focus: Christian meditation primarily focuses on:

Divine Presence: The core of Christian meditation is the awareness and experience of the presence of God. It emphasizes communion with the divine through silence, contemplation, and prayer.

Scripture Reflection: In some Christian meditation practices, the focus is on reading, reflecting on, and applying passages from the Bible to one's life.

Silence and Stillness: Silence and stillness are essential elements of Christian meditation, allowing practitioners to create a receptive space for divine communication.

Listening and Receptivity: The practice encourages listening to God's presence and being receptive to divine guidance and communication without seeking specific outcomes.

Christian meditation is a deeply personal and spiritual practice that varies among individuals and Christian denominations. It can be adapted to fit one's beliefs, preferences, and spiritual journey. The goal is to cultivate a deeper, more intimate relationship with God and to experience His presence in the stillness of the heart and mind.

Yoga in Relation to Meditation: Exploring Origins, Benefits on Mind and Body

Yoga and meditation are two ancient practices that have been intertwined for centuries, offering profound benefits to the mind and body. While yoga encompasses a holistic system of physical postures, breath control, ethical principles, and meditation techniques, this discussion will focus on the relationship between yoga and meditation, their historical origins, and the extensive benefits they offer for mental and physical well-being.

Origins of Yoga and Meditation

Yoga's Ancient Roots: Yoga has its origins in ancient India and can be traced back over 5,000 years. It emerged as a spiritual and philosophical discipline within the Indus Valley civilization and later evolved through various texts and traditions. The earliest known reference to yoga can be found in the sacred Indian texts called the Vedas, which date back to around 1500 BCE. Yoga was later systematized and codified in texts like the Yoga Sutras of Patanjali, which is often considered a foundational text for classical yoga.

Meditation's Early Beginnings: Meditation, like yoga, has a rich history rooted in various spiritual and philosophical traditions across the world. In India, meditation practices were developed and refined alongside yoga. The Vedic texts contain references to meditative practices, and meditation techniques were further elaborated upon in texts like the Upanishads and the Bhagavad Gita. Jainism and Buddhism, two other Indian traditions, also contributed to the development and spread of meditation practices.

The Relationship Between Yoga and Meditation: The relationship between yoga and meditation is intricate and symbiotic. While yoga encompasses a wide range of physical postures (asanas), breath control exercises (pranayama), ethical guidelines (yamas and niyamas), and meditation techniques, meditation is a specific aspect of yoga that focuses on cultivating mindfulness, inner awareness, and spiritual growth.

Types of Meditation in Yoga: Within the context of yoga, meditation takes various forms, each with its own techniques and objectives. Some of the most commonly practiced forms of meditation within yoga include:

Dhyana (Concentration Meditation): This type of meditation involves focusing the mind on a single point of concentration, such as a mantra, the breath, or an object. The goal is to achieve sustained concentration and a deep state of absorption.

Japa Meditation: Japa involves the repetition of a sacred mantra or phrase. The practitioner repeats the mantra silently or audibly, allowing it to permeate their consciousness and lead to deeper states of awareness.

Loving-Kindness Meditation (Metta): Metta meditation focuses on cultivating feelings of loving-kindness and compassion for oneself and others. It involves repeating phrases or affirmations that promote love, well-being, and goodwill.

Chakra Meditation: Chakra meditation involves visualizing and meditating on the body's energy centers (chakras) to promote balance, healing, and spiritual growth.

Yoga Nidra (Yogic Sleep): Yoga Nidra is a guided meditation technique that induces deep relaxation and a state of conscious sleep. It is often used for stress reduction and emotional healing.

Benefits of Yoga and Meditation on the Mind and Body

Mental Benefits:

Stress Reduction: Both yoga and meditation are renowned for their stress-reducing effects. The practice of mindful awareness in meditation helps individuals respond to stressors with equanimity, while yoga postures release physical tension, calming the nervous system.

Improved Concentration: Meditation, particularly concentration meditation, enhances focus and concentration by training the mind to remain on a single point of attention. This translates into improved productivity and mental clarity in daily life.

Emotional Regulation: Meditation, especially loving-kindness meditation, helps individuals recognize and manage their emotions more effectively. Yoga postures can also facilitate emotional release and balance.

Enhanced Self-Awareness: Both yoga and meditation encourage self-reflection and introspection. This heightened self-awareness can lead to personal growth, better decision-making, and increased emotional intelligence.

Reduction in Anxiety and Depression: Numerous studies have shown that regular yoga and meditation practice can reduce symptoms of anxiety and depression. Mindfulness meditation, in particular, has been incorporated into clinical therapies for these conditions.

Greater Resilience: Yoga and meditation can enhance psychological resilience, helping individuals bounce back from setbacks and challenges more easily.

Physical Benefits:

Flexibility and Strength: Yoga postures promote flexibility and strength throughout the body. Regular practice can improve muscle tone and prevent injuries.

Improved Posture: Many yoga poses emphasize proper alignment and balance, which can lead to better posture and reduced musculoskeletal pain.

Pain Relief: Yoga has been shown to alleviate chronic pain conditions such as lower back pain, arthritis, and migraines. Meditation can also reduce pain perception and improve pain management.

Enhanced Breathing: Pranayama, the practice of breath control in yoga, strengthens respiratory muscles and improves lung function. Proper breathing techniques can reduce stress and increase energy levels.

Cardiovascular Health: Meditation and yoga have been linked to improvements in heart health. They can reduce blood pressure, lower cholesterol levels, and decrease the risk of heart disease.

Better Sleep: Mindfulness meditation, relaxation techniques, and yoga nidra can improve sleep quality and help individuals with insomnia or sleep disorders.

Spiritual Benefits:

Connection to the Divine: Both yoga and meditation are paths to spiritual growth and self-realization. They offer opportunities to connect with one's inner self and experience a sense of oneness with the universe or the divine.

Cultivation of Inner Peace: Meditation, in particular, fosters inner peace and contentment. The practice of letting go of attachments and desires aligns with spiritual principles found in many traditions.

Deepened Faith: For many practitioners, yoga and meditation are integral to their spiritual journeys and religious beliefs. They can deepen one's faith and sense of purpose.

Yoga and meditation are ancient practices that have stood the test of time, offering a wide range of benefits for the mind, body, and spirit. Their interplay, as found in various forms of meditation within yoga, demonstrates their complementary nature. From reducing stress and improving mental clarity to enhancing physical health and fostering spiritual growth, the combination of yoga and meditation is a powerful tool for holistic well-being. Whether pursued for physical fitness, mental peace, or spiritual awakening, the practices of yoga and meditation continue to enrich the lives of countless individuals across the globe.

Preparing for Meditation

Meditation is a transformative practice that offers numerous physical, mental, and emotional benefits. However, the effectiveness of meditation often depends on how well you prepare for it. Preparing for meditation involves creating the right environment, adopting the proper mindset, and choosing the most suitable techniques to align with your goals. In this comprehensive guide, we will explore the essential steps to prepare for meditation, ensuring a successful and enriching practice.

The Importance of Preparation

Before delving into the specific steps of preparation, it's essential to understand why it's crucial. Preparation sets the stage for a successful meditation session by addressing physical comfort, mental readiness, and environmental factors. Here are some key reasons why preparation matters:

Enhanced Focus: Proper preparation helps you settle into your meditation practice with a clear and focused mind, reducing distractions and restlessness.

Physical Comfort: Physical comfort ensures that you can sit or lie down for an extended period without discomfort, allowing you to remain still and attentive.

Effective Relaxation: Adequate preparation allows you to release physical tension and mental clutter, making it easier to enter a state of deep relaxation and inner peace.

Consistency: Establishing a preparation routine creates a sense of ritual and consistency in your meditation practice, reinforcing its importance and making it easier to integrate into your daily life.

Goal Alignment: Preparing for meditation enables you to choose techniques and approaches that align with your specific goals, whether it's stress reduction, self-discovery, or spiritual growth.

Now, let's explore the steps involved in preparing for meditation:

Choose a Suitable Meditation Technique:

The first step in preparing for meditation is to select a meditation technique that resonates with your intentions and preferences. There are various meditation styles, each with its unique focus and approach. Here are some popular meditation techniques:

Mindfulness Meditation: Focuses on cultivating present-moment awareness by observing thoughts, emotions, and sensations without judgment.

Concentration Meditation: Involves concentrating on a single point of focus, such as the breath, a mantra, or a visual object, to develop deep concentration and mental clarity.

Loving-Kindness Meditation (Metta): Promotes feelings of love and compassion for oneself and others, often using affirmations and visualizations.

Body Scan Meditation: Involves systematically scanning and relaxing the body, releasing tension and promoting physical and mental relaxation.

Transcendental Meditation (TM): Utilizes a specific mantra-based technique to reach a unique state of restful awareness and self-transcendence.

Chakra Meditation: Focuses on the body's energy centers (chakras) to balance and harmonize physical and energetic aspects.

Select a technique that resonates with your goals and preferences. If you're new to meditation, experimenting with different methods can help you find the one that suits you best.

Create a Sacred Space:

Having a dedicated space for meditation enhances the sense of ritual and focus. Create a sacred meditation space within your home, no matter how small. Here's how:

Choose a Quiet Location: Find a quiet corner or room where you won't be easily disturbed. If you're unable to secure a quiet space, consider using noise-canceling headphones or a white noise machine.

Arrange Comfortable Seating: Ensure you have a comfortable chair, cushion, or meditation bench. Maintaining an upright yet relaxed posture is essential for extended meditation sessions.

Decorate Mindfully: Decorate your space with items that inspire you, such as candles, incense, a small altar, or meaningful artwork. These can create a serene atmosphere and deepen your sense of sacredness.

Minimize Distractions: Remove or minimize distractions like electronic devices, clutter, or loud decorations. The goal is to create a serene environment conducive to meditation.

Choose the Right Time:

The timing of your meditation practice can significantly impact its effectiveness. Select a time that aligns with your energy levels and daily routine. Here are some considerations:

Morning Meditation: Many people find that meditating in the morning helps set a positive tone for the day. The mind is often fresh, and there are fewer external distractions.

Evening Meditation: Evening meditation can be beneficial for unwinding and releasing the day's stress. It can also improve sleep quality.

Consistency Matters: Choose a consistent time for your daily meditation practice. Consistency reinforces the habit and maximizes its benefits.

Dress Comfortably:

Wearing comfortable clothing is essential for a meditation practice. Choose loose-fitting, breathable garments that allow you to sit or lie down without restriction. Remove any accessories or items that may cause discomfort, such as tight belts or jewelry.

Set Realistic Expectations:

Understanding that meditation is a skill that develops over time can help you manage expectations. Don't anticipate immediate results or complete mental silence. Meditation is about cultivating awareness and presence, which may take time and patience.

Empty Your Bladder and Stomach:

Before beginning your meditation, it's a good idea to visit the restroom to empty your bladder. A full bladder can be distracting during meditation. Additionally, avoid heavy meals or stimulants like caffeine immediately before meditating, as they may hinder relaxation.

Warm-Up and Stretch:

Light stretching or yoga asanas can prepare your body for meditation by releasing physical tension and promoting relaxation. A brief warm-up routine can help you sit comfortably and maintain a relaxed posture during meditation.

Set an Intention:

Before starting your meditation, take a moment to set an intention or purpose for your practice. This intention can guide your focus and create a sense of purpose. It might be to cultivate inner peace, reduce stress, gain insight, or be present.

Silence and Turn Off Devices:

Ensure that your meditation environment is free from distractions. Turn off or silence your phone and any other electronic devices that may interrupt your practice. You can also consider using a timer to avoid checking the clock during meditation.

Mindful Transition:

As you transition into meditation, do so mindfully. Take a few deep breaths, and consciously leave behind the concerns and busyness of the day. Let go of any mental baggage and arrive fully in the present moment.

Begin Your Meditation:

Start your chosen meditation technique, whether it involves focusing on your breath, repeating a mantra, or any other method. Maintain a gentle and non-judgmental awareness of your chosen point of focus.

Be Open to the Experience:

As you meditate, remain open and receptive to whatever arises—thoughts, emotions, sensations, or insights. Avoid striving for a particular outcome or resisting what emerges. Allow your meditation to unfold naturally.

Post-Meditation Reflection:

After completing your meditation, take a few moments to reflect on your experience. Notice how you feel mentally, emotionally, and physically. Journaling your thoughts and insights can be a valuable practice to deepen your understanding of your meditation experiences over time.

Preparing for meditation is a vital aspect of the practice that enhances its effectiveness and allows you to fully reap its benefits. By carefully selecting a suitable technique, creating a conducive environment, and adopting a mindful approach, you can embark on a rewarding meditation journey. Remember that meditation is a lifelong practice, and each session contributes to your personal growth and well-being. Embrace the process with patience and an open heart, and you'll discover the transformative power of meditation in your life.

Importance and Benefits of Proper Posture and Breath Control in Meditation:

Proper posture and breath control are foundational aspects of meditation practice. They provide a stable foundation for your meditation, facilitate physical comfort, and enhance mental focus. Understanding their importance and the benefits they offer is crucial for developing a successful and enriching meditation practice.

Importance of Proper Posture:

Physical Comfort: Maintaining an appropriate meditation posture ensures physical comfort during your practice. Discomfort or pain in your body can become a significant distraction, making it challenging to focus on your meditation object or technique.

Alignment: Proper posture promotes the alignment of your spine, allowing for the unobstructed flow of energy throughout your body. This alignment contributes to overall physical well-being.

Stability: A stable posture, whether sitting or lying down, helps anchor your body and mind. It provides a sense of grounding that makes it easier to remain still and attentive during meditation.

Preventing Distractions: Physical discomfort or an unstable posture can lead to restlessness and fidgeting, creating distractions that hinder the depth of your meditation practice.

Enhancing Breath Control: Proper posture supports optimal breathing, allowing you to engage in effective breath control techniques that promote relaxation and focus.

Benefits of Proper Posture:

Improved Concentration: A stable and comfortable posture allows you to concentrate more effectively during meditation. It minimizes the physical distractions that can disrupt your focus.

Relaxation: Proper posture promotes relaxation in your muscles and joints. This physical relaxation extends to the mind, helping to ease mental tension and stress.

Deeper Meditation: When your body is at ease, you're more likely to experience deeper meditation sessions. A comfortable posture facilitates a smoother transition into altered states of consciousness and heightened awareness.

Mind-Body Connection: Proper posture enhances the connection between your body and mind. You become more attuned to your body's sensations and can use this awareness as a meditation anchor.

Physical Health: Consistent practice of proper posture in meditation can have long-term benefits for your physical health, including improved posture in your everyday life.

Importance of Breath Control:

Calming the Nervous System: Breath control techniques, such as diaphragmatic breathing, activate the parasympathetic nervous system, inducing a state of relaxation and reducing the "fight or flight" response.

Enhancing Mindfulness: Focusing on your breath provides a tangible and ever-present point of attention. It enhances mindfulness, helping you observe thoughts, emotions, and sensations without judgment.

Stress Reduction: Controlled breathing can significantly reduce stress and anxiety. It regulates the release of stress hormones and induces a sense of calm.

Improved Oxygenation: Proper breath control ensures efficient oxygen exchange in the body, increasing overall energy levels and mental clarity.

Emotional Regulation: Breath control techniques can help regulate emotions by providing a means to pause and respond consciously rather than reacting impulsively to emotional triggers.

Benefits of Breath Control:

Enhanced Concentration: Breath control techniques help sharpen your focus during meditation. The rhythmic nature of controlled breathing can anchor your awareness and reduce mental chatter.

Stress Reduction: Controlled breathing is a potent tool for managing stress and anxiety. It allows you to control your body's physiological response to stressors.

Emotional Balance: By regulating your breath, you can gain better control over your emotional responses. This can lead to greater emotional resilience and well-being.

Improved Lung Function: Breath control exercises strengthen respiratory muscles and enhance lung capacity. This can improve overall lung function and oxygenation of the body.

Mindfulness Development: Breath control and mindfulness are closely connected. Consistent practice of breath control naturally deepens your mindfulness skills, helping you become more present in your daily life.

Incorporating Proper Posture and Breath Control into Your Meditation Practice:

Select a Comfortable Posture: Choose a posture that suits your body and flexibility level. Common meditation postures include sitting on a cushion, chair, or floor, or lying down. Ensure your back is straight but not rigid, and your shoulders are relaxed.

Mindful Alignment: Pay attention to the alignment of your spine and the positioning of your head. Imagine a string pulling you gently upward from the crown of your head, aligning your spine.

Regular Stretching: Engage in light stretching or yoga asanas before your meditation to release physical tension and prepare your body for stillness.

Breath Awareness: Begin your meditation with a few moments of breath awareness. Observe your natural breath without trying to control it. This can help you transition into focused breath control if desired.

Practice Breath Control Techniques: Explore different breath control techniques that resonate with you, such as diaphragmatic breathing, deep belly breathing, or alternate nostril breathing. Incorporate these techniques as part of your meditation practice to enhance relaxation and concentration.

Progress Gradually: If you're new to breath control, start with short sessions and gradually extend the duration as you become more comfortable with the techniques.

Seek Guidance: Consider learning breath control techniques from experienced meditation teachers or through guided meditation apps or resources. Proper guidance can enhance your practice and understanding.

Consistency: Incorporate proper posture and breath control into your meditation practice consistently. Regularity reinforces these fundamental aspects and deepens their benefits over time.

Proper posture and breath control are fundamental elements of a successful meditation practice. They create a stable foundation for your meditation, facilitate physical comfort, enhance concentration, and promote relaxation and emotional well-being. By understanding their importance and consistently incorporating them into your practice, you can maximize the transformative power of meditation in your life.

Addressing Common Challenges of Meditation and Yoga: Strategies for Overcoming Obstacles

Meditation and yoga are powerful practices that offer numerous physical, mental, and spiritual benefits. However, like any transformative endeavor, they come with their share of challenges. Understanding and addressing these challenges is essential for establishing a consistent and rewarding practice. In this discussion, we will explore some of the common challenges encountered in meditation and yoga and provide strategies to overcome them.

Common Challenges in Meditation:

Restlessness and Racing Thoughts:

Challenge: One of the most prevalent challenges in meditation is a restless mind characterized by racing thoughts. It can be challenging to quiet the mind and maintain focus.

Solution: Overcoming this challenge requires patience and practice. Techniques such as mindfulness meditation, concentration meditation, or guided meditation can help by providing a specific point of focus for your attention. Acknowledge racing thoughts without judgment and gently bring your focus back to your chosen anchor, be it your breath, a mantra, or a visualization.

Physical Discomfort:

Challenge: Physical discomfort, such as stiffness, numbness, or pain, can arise during meditation, especially if you are sitting for an extended period.

Solution: Choose a comfortable meditation posture that suits your body. Experiment with different cushions, chairs, or meditation benches. Incorporate gentle stretching or yoga poses before meditation to release physical tension. If discomfort arises during meditation, adjust your posture mindfully without losing focus.

Inconsistent Practice:

Challenge: Maintaining a regular meditation practice can be challenging due to busy schedules, distractions, or lack of motivation.

Solution: Set realistic goals and create a consistent routine. Start with shorter sessions and gradually extend the duration as you build the habit. Choose a specific time and place for meditation to make it a part of your daily life. Use reminders or meditation apps to stay accountable.

Impatience and Expectations:

Challenge: Impatience and high expectations for immediate results can lead to frustration and disappointment in meditation.

Solution: Approach meditation with an open and patient mindset. Understand that meditation is a skill that develops over time. Let go of specific outcomes and focus on the process. Celebrate small improvements and moments of calm, rather than aiming for perfection.

Resistance to Emotions:

Challenge: Uncomfortable emotions, memories, or past traumas may surface during meditation, leading to resistance and aversion.

Solution: Embrace a compassionate attitude towards yourself and your experiences. Instead of pushing away difficult emotions, allow them to arise without judgment. Meditation can be a safe space for processing and healing. If emotions become overwhelming, seek support from a therapist or counselor.

Common Challenges in Yoga:

Physical Limitations:

Challenge: Physical limitations or injuries can hinder your yoga practice, making certain poses or movements uncomfortable or impossible.

Solution: Prioritize safety and listen to your body. Work with a knowledgeable yoga teacher who can provide modifications and adjustments to accommodate your physical limitations. Focus on poses and sequences that support your body's needs and gradually build strength and flexibility over time.

Self-Comparison:

Challenge: The yoga community, both in-person and online, can sometimes foster a culture of comparison, where practitioners feel pressure to perform advanced poses or achieve specific aesthetics.

Solution: Remember that yoga is a personal journey. Focus on your own progress and growth, rather than comparing yourself to others. Celebrate your achievements, no matter how small, and practice self-compassion. If social media triggers comparison, consider taking breaks or curating your online content to be more supportive of your journey.

Lack of Motivation:

Challenge: Staying motivated to practice yoga regularly can be challenging, especially during periods of low energy or busy schedules.

Solution: Cultivate intrinsic motivation by connecting with the deeper reasons you practice yoga. Reflect on how it makes you feel physically and mentally. Set realistic goals and break them into smaller, achievable steps. Find joy in your practice by exploring different styles of yoga or incorporating music, aromatherapy, or guided meditations.

Inflexibility:

Challenge: Feeling physically inflexible can be discouraging, particularly if you struggle with poses that require flexibility.

Solution: Accept where your body is at in its flexibility journey. Regular stretching and consistent yoga practice will gradually increase flexibility. Incorporate gentle and restorative poses into your practice to enhance flexibility safely. Patience is key; remember that yoga is about progress, not perfection.

Boredom or Plateau:

Challenge: Over time, you may feel that your yoga practice has plateaued or become repetitive, leading to boredom.

Solution: Keep your practice fresh and engaging by exploring new yoga styles, attending workshops or classes, or setting new goals. Challenge yourself with different poses or sequences, and consider the mental and emotional benefits of your practice. Yoga is not just physical; it's a holistic practice that encompasses mindfulness and self-discovery.

Strategies for Overcoming Challenges in Meditation and Yoga:

Consistent Practice: The most effective way to overcome challenges is to maintain a consistent practice. Regular meditation and yoga build resilience and deepen your understanding of yourself. Even on challenging days, show up to your practice, even if it's for a shorter session.

Seek Guidance: Consider working with experienced teachers or instructors who can offer guidance and support. They can provide personalized advice, modifications, and encouragement to help you navigate challenges.

Mindfulness and Self-Compassion: Cultivate mindfulness both on and off the mat or cushion. Use mindfulness to observe challenges as they arise without judgment. Practice self-compassion by treating yourself with kindness and understanding, especially when facing difficulties.

Adapt and Modify: Don't hesitate to adapt or modify your practice as needed. Whether it's adjusting your meditation technique or modifying yoga poses, prioritize safety and comfort.

Variety and Exploration: Keep your practice exciting by exploring different meditation techniques and yoga styles. Attend workshops or retreats to deepen your knowledge and experience new approaches.

Community and Support: Connect with like-minded individuals who share your challenges and goals. Joining a meditation group or yoga community can provide a sense of belonging and encouragement.

Reflect and Journal: Regularly reflect on your meditation and yoga experiences through journaling. Document your challenges, breakthroughs, and insights. This can help you gain clarity and track your progress.

Remember the Purpose: Revisit your reasons for practising meditation and yoga. Reconnecting with your intentions can reignite your motivation and remind you of the transformative potential of these practices.

Challenges are an integral part of the meditation and yoga journey. Instead of viewing them as obstacles, see them as opportunities for growth, self-discovery, and resilience. By adopting a patient, compassionate, and adaptable mindset, and by seeking support when needed, you can overcome these challenges and continue to experience the profound benefits of meditation and yoga in your life.

Remember that the path of meditation and yoga is a lifelong journey, and each challenge is a stepping stone towards greater self-awareness and well-being.

Part II: Exploring the Self

The journey of exploring the self is a profound and intricate odyssey that each of us embarks upon in our lifetime. It is an expedition into the depths of our consciousness, a quest to unravel the mysteries of our identity, motivations, and purpose. This journey holds the promise of self-realization, personal growth, and a deeper connection with the world around us. In this exploration, we navigate through the labyrinths of our thoughts, emotions, and experiences, seeking to answer age-old questions about who we are and what it means to be human.

The Labyrinth Within: The Complex Nature of the Self

Imagine the self as a vast and intricate labyrinth, with countless corridors and hidden chambers. Each corridor represents a facet of your personality, a layer of your identity, and every chamber conceals memories, desires, and emotions. As we step into this labyrinth, we encounter the complexity of the human experience. We confront our joys and sorrows, our strengths and vulnerabilities, and the paradoxes that define us. This inner journey is an expedition into the heart of this labyrinth, a quest to discover its secrets.

The Mirrored Self: Reflections in Relationships

Our interactions with others serve as mirrors that reflect facets of our own selves. The dynamics of relationships, whether they be with family, friends, or romantic partners, offer opportunities for self-exploration. Our reactions to people, the patterns we repeat, and the conflicts we encounter all provide clues to the hidden aspects of our psyche.

For instance, in moments of frustration with a loved one, we may uncover our own insecurities or unresolved issues. In moments of compassion, we glimpse the capacity for empathy within us. By paying attention to these reflections in our relationships, we can gain insights into our fears, desires, and the patterns that shape our interactions.

The Inner Dialogue: Conversations with Ourselves

Our inner dialogue is a continuous conversation we have with ourselves. It encompasses our thoughts, beliefs, and the stories we tell about our lives. This internal chatter can be both a source of wisdom and a wellspring of confusion. It is through introspection that we navigate this internal landscape.

One powerful technique for self-exploration is mindfulness meditation. By observing our thoughts without judgment, we gain clarity about the patterns and narratives that shape our perception of reality. We learn to differentiate between the stories we tell ourselves and the objective truth. In this way, meditation offers a path to understanding the self as it is, beyond the distortions of our internal dialogue.

The Shadows of the Self: Embracing the Darker Aspects

Exploring the self requires us to confront our shadows—the aspects of ourselves that we may be inclined to deny or hide. These shadows often contain our fears, insecurities, and repressed emotions. Carl Jung, the renowned Swiss psychiatrist, described the shadow as the "dark side" of the self, the hidden realm of our subconscious.

Confronting our shadows can be a daunting task, but it is essential for personal growth and self-acceptance. By acknowledging and embracing these hidden aspects, we integrate them into our conscious awareness, transforming them from sources of inner conflict into catalysts for personal transformation.

The Quest for Meaning: Seeking Purpose and Values

One of the central questions in the exploration of the self is the quest for meaning and purpose. What gives our lives significance, and what values guide our actions? This search often leads us to examine our beliefs, ideals, and the principles that govern our choices.

Philosophers, psychologists, and spiritual teachers have long contemplated the question of purpose. Viktor Frankl, a Holocaust survivor and psychiatrist, argued that finding meaning in suffering is essential for human well-being. He believed that each person has a unique purpose, and the search for that purpose is a fundamental part of the human experience.

The Journey Inward: Practices for Self-Exploration

While the journey of self-exploration is deeply personal and subjective, there are several practices and approaches that can aid in this quest:

Meditation and Mindfulness: As mentioned earlier, meditation and mindfulness offer valuable tools for introspection. They help us observe our thoughts, emotions, and sensations with a non-judgmental awareness, providing insight into our inner workings.

Journaling: Keeping a journal is a powerful way to record your thoughts, feelings, and reflections. Regular journaling can reveal patterns in your thinking and emotions, allowing you to delve deeper into your inner world.

Therapy and Counseling: Seeking the guidance of a trained therapist or counselor can provide a supportive and structured environment for self-exploration. Professionals can help you navigate through challenges, traumas, and unresolved issues.

Creative Expression: Art, writing, music, and other creative outlets can serve as mediums for self-expression and exploration. Creative endeavors often tap into the subconscious, bringing to light hidden emotions and insights.

Solitude and Retreats: Periods of solitude and retreats, whether in nature or in a contemplative setting, provide opportunities for introspection and self-discovery. They allow you to step away from the distractions of daily life and delve into your inner world.

The Never-Ending Journey: Embracing Change and Growth

The journey of exploring the self is not a destination but a continuous process. It is a path of self-acceptance, growth, and evolution. Just as the self is multifaceted, so too is the journey of self-exploration. It encompasses moments of joy and moments of discomfort, moments of clarity and moments of confusion.

As we navigate the labyrinth of the self, we uncover layers of understanding, shedding old beliefs and assumptions along the way. We learn to embrace impermanence and change, recognizing that the self is not static but ever-evolving.

Ultimately, the exploration of the self leads to a profound sense of self-acceptance and compassion. It is a journey of becoming intimately acquainted with who we are—the light and the shadow, the strengths and the vulnerabilities. In this journey, we discover that the self is a tapestry of experiences, emotions, and relationships, woven together in a unique and beautiful expression of human existence.

In closing, the exploration of the self is a sacred and transformative journey. It is an adventure into the depths of our consciousness, a quest for self-discovery, and a celebration of the multifaceted nature of our being. It is an invitation to embrace the complexity of our humanity and to embark on a lifelong journey of self-awareness, growth, and self-compassion

Self-Awareness and Mindfulness: The Path to Personal Growth and Well-Being

Self-awareness and mindfulness are two interconnected and powerful practices that play a profound role in our personal growth and well being. Together, they enable us to understand ourselves at a deeper level, cultivate emotional intelligence, and navigate life's challenges with greater resilience. In this exploration, we'll delve into the concepts of self-awareness and mindfulness, how they intersect, and the transformative benefits they offer.

Self-Awareness: The Foundation of Personal Growth

Self-awareness is the ability to introspectively and objectively observe one's thoughts, feelings, behaviors, and motivations. It's like shining a spotlight on the inner landscape of your mind and emotions, allowing you to gain a clearer understanding of who you are.

The Layers of Self-Awareness:

Cognitive Self-Awareness: This level involves recognizing your thoughts and beliefs. It's about understanding the stories you tell yourself and the narratives that shape your perception of the world.

Emotional Self-Awareness: Emotional self-awareness involves identifying and understanding your emotions as they arise. It allows you to recognize not only what you're feeling but also why you're feeling that way.

Behavioral Self-Awareness: This aspect focuses on your actions and behaviors. It involves observing how your thoughts and emotions influence your behavior and how your behavior, in turn, affects your thoughts and emotions.

Motivational Self-Awareness: Motivational self-awareness delves into the deeper layers of your desires, values, and long-term goals. It helps you understand what truly motivates you and drives your choices.

The Benefits of Self-Awareness:

Enhanced Emotional Regulation: Self-awareness allows you to recognize emotional triggers and respond to them with greater control and mindfulness. It reduces impulsive reactions and fosters emotional resilience.

Improved Decision-Making: When you understand your values, beliefs, and motivations, you can make decisions that align with your authentic self, leading to greater satisfaction and fulfillment.

Better Relationships: Self-awareness enhances your capacity for empathy and understanding in relationships. It enables you to communicate more effectively and resolve conflicts with greater empathy.

Reduced Stress: Recognizing the sources of stress in your life and how you react to them empowers you to manage stress more effectively.

Personal Growth: Self-awareness is the foundation of personal growth and self-improvement. It allows you to identify areas for development and take intentional steps toward positive change.

Mindfulness: Cultivating Presence and Awareness

Mindfulness is the practice of being fully present in the moment, with an open and non-judgmental awareness of your thoughts, emotions, sensations, and the world around you. It involves paying attention to your experiences as they unfold, without attachment or aversion.

Key Aspects of Mindfulness:

Present-Moment Awareness: Mindfulness encourages you to bring your attention to the here and now. It involves noticing the sensations of your breath, the sounds around you, or the taste of your food in a state of complete presence.

Non-Judgmental Awareness: In mindfulness, you observe your thoughts, emotions, and sensations without judgment. You acknowledge them as they are, recognizing that there is no "right" or "wrong" way to feel or think.

Acceptance: Mindfulness involves accepting your experiences, whether pleasant or unpleasant, with equanimity. It's about letting go of resistance and allowing things to be as they are.

Purposeful Attention: Mindfulness requires intention and effort. It involves consciously directing your attention to the chosen focal point, which could be your breath, bodily sensations, or a specific object.

The Benefits of Mindfulness:

Stress Reduction: Mindfulness practices, such as mindfulness meditation, have been shown to reduce stress and promote relaxation. By focusing on the present moment, you can break the cycle of rumination and worry.

Improved Mental Health: Mindfulness is effective in managing conditions like anxiety, depression, and PTSD. It helps individuals gain distance from their thoughts and emotions, reducing their impact.

Enhanced Concentration: Regular mindfulness practice enhances your ability to concentrate and sustain attention. It sharpens your cognitive abilities and enhances mental clarity.

Emotional Regulation: Mindfulness allows you to observe your emotions without reacting impulsively. It creates a space between stimulus and response, giving you greater control over your reactions.

Greater Resilience: Mindfulness fosters resilience by helping you approach life's challenges with equanimity and adaptability. It allows you to navigate difficulties with a calm and clear mind.

The Synergy Between Self-Awareness and Mindfulness:

Self-awareness and mindfulness are interconnected practices that complement each other in various ways:

Self-Reflection Through Mindfulness: Mindfulness provides a platform for self-reflection and self-awareness. When you observe your thoughts and emotions without judgment, you gain insights into your cognitive and emotional patterns.

Enhanced Emotional Intelligence: The self-awareness gained through mindfulness deepens emotional intelligence. You become attuned to your emotions, recognizing their nuances and understanding their origins.

Self-Compassion: Mindfulness cultivates self-compassion by encouraging non-judgmental self-observation. As you become more self-aware, you are better equipped to treat yourself with kindness and understanding.

Intentional Living: Mindfulness helps you live with intention and purpose by bringing awareness to your choices and behaviors. It aligns your actions with your values and motivations, enhancing self-aware decision-making.

Stress Reduction: The stress-reducing benefits of mindfulness can indirectly enhance self-awareness. Reduced stress levels create a calmer mental environment for introspection and self-observation.

Incorporating Self-Awareness and Mindfulness into Daily Life:

Mindful Activities: Infuse mindfulness into everyday activities. Whether you're eating, walking, or working, approach these tasks with full presence and awareness.

Journaling: Keep a journal to record your thoughts, emotions, and reflections. Regular journaling can deepen self-awareness and provide a record of your mindfulness journey.

Meditation: Practice mindfulness meditation regularly. Start with short sessions and gradually extend the duration as you build your practice. Guided meditations can also be helpful for beginners.

Mindful Breathing: Engage in mindful breathing exercises throughout the day. Take a few conscious breaths when you feel stressed or overwhelmed to center yourself in the present moment.

Self-Reflective Questions: Ask yourself self-reflective questions regularly. For example, "What am I feeling right now?" or "What are the underlying beliefs driving my actions?"

Seek Guidance: Consider joining mindfulness or meditation groups or seeking the guidance of a mindfulness teacher or therapist. Community and support can enhance your practice.

Conclusion: The Journey of Self-Awareness and Mindfulness

The journey of self-awareness and mindfulness is a profound exploration of the inner self and the present moment. Together, these practices empower you to navigate life's complexities with greater clarity, equanimity, and compassion. They invite you to delve into the layers of your identity, understand your emotions, and cultivate a deeper connection with yourself and the world around you.

In this journey, you become both the observer and the observed, gaining profound insights into your thoughts, emotions, and behaviors. You discover that true self-awareness is not about changing who you are but about embracing and understanding yourself more fully. It is a journey of self-acceptance, growth, and the awakening of your highest potential.

As you integrate self-awareness and mindfulness into your daily life, you embark on a transformative path towards greater well-being, emotional intelligence, and a profound sense of presence in each moment. The journey is ongoing, and its rewards are boundless, offering a lifelong exploration of the depths of your inner world and the richness of the present moment

Cultivating Self-Awareness Through Meditation: A Journey Within

Self-awareness is the cornerstone of personal growth and well-being. It's the ability to understand your thoughts, emotions, and behaviors, to recognize your strengths and weaknesses, and to navigate life with clarity and authenticity. Meditation is a powerful tool for cultivating self-awareness, offering a journey within that allows you to explore the depths of your consciousness. In this exploration, we'll delve into how meditation can be used as a transformative practice for enhancing self-awareness.

The Essence of Meditation:

Meditation is a practice of focused attention and awareness. It involves training the mind to become still and observant, allowing you to explore your inner world with greater clarity. While there are various meditation techniques, the fundamental principles remain consistent:

Attention: Meditation directs your attention to a specific point of focus. This might be your breath, a mantra, a visual object, or even your thoughts and emotions themselves. This chosen focus serves as an anchor for your awareness.

Observation: With sustained attention, you begin to observe the contents of your mind without attachment or judgment. You become a witness to your thoughts, feelings, and sensations as they arise and pass away.

Non-Judgment: A key aspect of meditation is non-judgmental awareness. Instead of labeling thoughts as "good" or "bad," you observe them impartially, recognizing that they are transient mental events.

Cultivating Self-Awareness Through Meditation:

Observing Thought Patterns:

Meditation allows you to witness the flow of your thoughts. You become aware of recurring thought patterns, whether they're related to self-doubt, worry, or judgment. By observing these patterns without attachment, you gain insights into your mental habits and conditioning.

Practice: During meditation, notice the thoughts that arise. Are they future-oriented, dwelling on the past, or centered in the present? Are they predominantly positive or negative? Observing these patterns helps you understand your thought landscape.

Exploring Emotional Responses:

Through meditation, you can explore your emotional responses with greater clarity. When emotions arise during your practice, you have the opportunity to observe them in their raw form. You may notice physical sensations accompanying emotions, such as tension or warmth.

Practice: When you experience an emotion during meditation, focus your awareness on the sensation in your body. Is there tightness in your chest with anxiety? Or a sense of ease and lightness with joy? This allows you to connect emotions with bodily sensations.

Uncovering the Ego:

Meditation provides insight into the nature of the ego, the sense of "I" or "me" that we identify with. As you observe your thoughts and emotions, you may notice how they create and reinforce your self-identity. This awareness can lead to a deeper understanding of the ego's role in your life.

Practice: During meditation, ask yourself, "Who is the one observing these thoughts and emotions?" This inquiry can lead you beyond the ego's identification with thoughts and towards a more expansive sense of self.

Recognizing Resistance:

Resistance often arises when faced with challenging thoughts or emotions. Meditation allows you to observe resistance as it occurs, shedding light on areas where you may be avoiding or denying aspects of yourself.

Practice: When resistance arises during meditation (e.g., a desire to end the session), take a moment to observe it. What does resistance feel like in your body? Is it a sensation of restlessness, discomfort, or tension? Understanding resistance can lead to greater self-acceptance.

Cultivating Presence:

At its core, meditation is a practice of presence. By training your mind to stay focused on the present moment, you develop a heightened awareness of your immediate experience. This presence extends beyond your meditation cushion and into your everyday life.

Practice: Use mindfulness meditation techniques to anchor your attention in the present moment. Focus on your breath, bodily sensations, or the sounds around you. When your mind wanders, gently bring it back to your chosen point of focus.

Challenges in Cultivating Self-Awareness Through Meditation:

Impatience and Frustration: It's common to become impatient or frustrated when you can't immediately access deep self-awareness through meditation. Remember that self-awareness is a gradual process, and each session contributes to your understanding.

Resistance to Uncomfortable Insights: Meditation may bring to light uncomfortable truths or unresolved issues. Instead of resisting these insights, approach them with curiosity and compassion. Consider seeking support from a therapist or counselor if needed.

Inconsistent Practice: Maintaining a consistent meditation practice can be challenging. Establishing a routine and setting realistic goals can help you overcome this challenge.

The Transformative Power of Self-Awareness:

Cultivating self-awareness through meditation is a transformative journey. As you deepen your understanding of yourself, you gain the capacity to:

Make Informed Choices: Self-awareness empowers you to make choices that align with your values and aspirations. It allows you to respond to situations rather than react impulsively.

Enhance Relationships: With greater self-awareness, you become more attuned to your emotions and better equipped to navigate interpersonal dynamics with empathy and understanding.

Manage Stress: Self-awareness helps you recognize the sources of stress in your life and develop effective coping strategies. It promotes emotional regulation and resilience.

Foster Personal Growth: Understanding your thought patterns, emotional responses, and behavioral tendencies opens the door to personal growth and self-improvement. You can intentionally work on areas you wish to develop.

Experience Greater Fulfillment: Ultimately, self-awareness leads to a deeper sense of fulfillment and contentment. It allows you to live authentically and in alignment with your true self.

In conclusion, self-awareness is a journey of exploration and discovery that meditation facilitates. It's a journey that invites you to know yourself on a profound level, to embrace your strengths and vulnerabilities, and to navigate life with wisdom and authenticity. Through regular meditation practice, you embark on an inner voyage that holds the potential for transformation and a deeper connection to your true self

Mindful Living in Daily Life: Cultivating Presence and Well-Being

Mindful living is a practice of bringing focused awareness and presence to your daily activities, interactions, and experiences. It involves consciously paying attention to the present moment, approaching each situation with an open and non-judgmental mindset. By integrating mindfulness into your everyday life, you can enhance your overall well-being, reduce stress, and foster a deeper sense of connection to yourself and the world around you.

Principles of Mindful Living:

Present-Moment Awareness: Mindful living centers on being fully present in the moment. Instead of dwelling on the past or worrying about the future, you engage with your current experience with undivided attention.

Non-Judgmental Observation: Mindfulness encourages you to observe your thoughts, emotions, and sensations without judgment. You acknowledge them as they are, without labeling them as "good" or "bad."

Acceptance and Compassion: Mindful living fosters an attitude of acceptance and self-compassion. It involves treating yourself and others with kindness, understanding that imperfections and challenges are part of the human experience.

Intentional Action: It emphasizes making intentional choices and actions aligned with your values and priorities. Mindful living encourages you to respond to situations consciously rather than reacting impulsively.

Practical Ways to Incorporate Mindful Living:

Mindful Breathing: Incorporate mindful breathing into your daily routine. Take moments to focus on your breath, even for a few minutes. This practice can be done while waiting in line, during a break, or before important meetings. Mindful breathing helps anchor you in the present moment, reducing stress and promoting clarity.

Mindful Eating: Pay close attention to your meals. Avoid distractions like smartphones or television. Savor each bite, notice the flavors and textures, and be fully present with the act of eating.

Mindful eating can lead to healthier food choices and improved digestion.

Mindful Walking: While walking, particularly in natural settings, practice walking mindfully. Feel the sensation of your feet touching the ground, notice the movement of your body, and be aware of the environment around you. This practice connects you to the beauty of the world and enhances your sense of presence.

Mindful Listening: When engaged in conversations, practice mindful listening. Give your full attention to the speaker without interrupting or formulating your response in your mind. Listen not only to words but also to tone, emotions, and body language. Mindful listening deepens your connections with others and promotes empathy.

Mindful Work: Apply mindfulness to your work routine. Before starting a task, take a moment to set your intention and focus on the task at hand. Minimize multitasking and distractions. Break tasks into smaller, manageable steps, and approach each step with mindful attention.

Mindful Self-Care: Dedicate time to self-care practices, such as meditation, yoga, or relaxation exercises. These activities allow you to reconnect with yourself, reduce stress, and promote emotional well-being.

Mindful Technology Use: Mindfully engage with technology. Be conscious of how and why you use your devices. Set boundaries for screen time, and practice digital detoxes regularly to unplug and recharge.

Mindful Gratitude: Cultivate a daily gratitude practice. Reflect on the things, people, or experiences you're grateful for. This practice shifts your focus toward positivity and enhances your overall well-being.

Mindful Responses to Stress: When faced with stress or challenging situations, take a moment to pause and breathe mindfully before responding. This brief pause can help you regain composure, make more thoughtful choices, and reduce emotional reactivity.

Overcoming Challenges in Mindful Living:

Mind Wandering: It's common for the mind to wander, especially when you're new to mindfulness. When this happens, gently redirect your focus back to the present moment without self-criticism.

Impatience: Mindful living is a gradual process, and the benefits may not be immediately apparent. Practice patience and remind yourself that each moment of awareness contributes to your overall well-being.

Inconsistent Practice: Maintaining a consistent mindful living practice can be challenging. Create reminders or establish a routine to make it a part of your daily life.

Benefits of Mindful Living:

Reduced Stress: Mindful living helps you respond to stressors with greater calmness and resilience. It reduces rumination and worry, allowing you to stay present in the face of challenges.

Improved Mental Health: Mindfulness has been shown to be effective in managing conditions like anxiety, depression, and PTSD. It enhances emotional regulation and reduces symptoms of distress.

Enhanced Focus and Productivity: Mindful living sharpens your ability to concentrate and sustain attention. This can lead to increased productivity and improved performance in various areas of your life.

Better Relationships: Mindful living fosters empathetic listening and effective communication. It promotes healthier interactions and deeper connections with others.

Greater Self-Awareness: Mindful living leads to a deeper understanding of yourself, your thoughts, emotions, and values. It supports personal growth and self-improvement.

Enhanced Well-Being: Ultimately, mindful living promotes overall well-being. It helps you find joy and contentment in the present moment, leading to a more fulfilling and meaningful life.

Living mindfully is a life-changing approach that encourages you to interact with your existence in a more deliberate and significant manner. By nurturing attentiveness and consciousness in everyday tasks, you can diminish stress, enhance your psychological well-being, and develop a stronger bond with your inner self and your surroundings. With regular application, living mindfully evolves into a habitual way of being, leading you to improved wellness and a more satisfying life.

Discovering Your True Essence

"Embarking on the quest 'Discovering Your True Essence' means undertaking a deep and introspective expedition into the self. This journey calls upon you to carefully dismantle the complex tapestry of conditioning, societal norms, and external expectations that have, over time, obscured the fundamental nature of your identity. It's not merely about shedding the superficial personas we frequently assume in reaction to the world's demands, but it's an invitation to a more profound and radical transformation. As you traverse deeper beneath these surface-level constructs, you start to reveal the purest part of who you are. This exploration is not for the faint of heart; it is an intensive process that requires courage and honesty. By engaging in this search, you gradually forge a pathway to a more genuine connection with the essence of your being, allowing you to embrace and embody your authentic self with clarity and confidence."

Understanding Your True Essence:

Beyond Roles and Labels: Your true essence is not defined by the roles you play or the labels society assigns to you. It transcends the masks you wear in different situations, such as being a parent, a professional, or a friend. Discovering your true essence involves peeling away these external identities to reveal your authentic self underneath.

Unearthing Core Values and Beliefs: Your true essence is closely tied to your core values and beliefs—the principles that guide your decisions and actions. It's about understanding what truly matters to you, what you stand for, and what you aspire to be. This exploration helps you align your life with your deepest convictions.

Connecting with Inner Wisdom: Your true essence is not something you need to acquire; it's already within you. It's the source of your intuition, inner wisdom, and authenticity. Discovering it involves quieting the noise of external influences and learning to listen to your inner voice.

The Path to Discovering Your True Essence:

Self-Reflection Start by setting aside time for self-reflection. Journaling, meditation, or quiet contemplation can help you explore your thoughts, feelings, and beliefs. Reflect on your life experiences, values, and what brings you a sense of fulfillment.

Questioning Assumptions: Challenge the assumptions and beliefs that have shaped your identity. Ask yourself why you hold certain beliefs or why you pursue specific goals. Are they aligned with your true essence, or do external pressures influence the?

Embracing Vulnerability: Vulnerability is a gateway to authenticity. Embrace your vulnerabilities and imperfections. They are part of what makes you unique. By accepting and owning them, you reveal more of your true self.

Seeking Inner Guidance: Practice mindfulness and introspection to connect with your inner wisdom. Pay attention to your intuition and gut feelings. Trust that you have the answers within you and allow your inner guidance to lead the way.

Exploring Passions and Interests: Engage in activities that ignite your passion and bring you joy. Pursue interests that resonate with your true essence. When you immerse yourself in what you love, you align more closely with your authentic self.

Cultivating Self-Compassion: Be gentle and compassionate with yourself throughout this journey. Self-discovery can be challenging, and it's okay to encounter resistance or discomfort. Treat yourself with the same kindness you would offer a dear friend.

Challenges in Discovering Your True Essence:

External Expectations: Society often imposes expectations and norms that can obscure your true essence. Overcoming these external pressures requires self-awareness and the courage to be yourself.

Fear of Rejection: The fear of not being accepted or valued for who you truly are can be a significant barrier. It takes bravery to step into your authenticity, even when it means risking rejection.

Past Conditioning: Past experiences and conditioning can create beliefs and patterns that don't align with your true essence. Overcoming these patterns may involve unraveling old conditioning and adopting new, more authentic beliefs.

Benefits of Discovering Your True Essence:

Authenticity: Discovering your true essence allows you to live authentically, embracing who you are at your core without pretense or conformity.

Clarity and Purpose: Understanding your values and beliefs provides clarity and purpose in life. You can make decisions that align with your true self, leading to greater fulfillment.

Improved Relationships: Authenticity fosters deeper and more meaningful connections. When you show up as your true self, you attract people who appreciate and accept you for who you are.

Inner Peace: Embracing your true essence often leads to a sense of inner peace and contentment. You're no longer striving to be someone you're not, but instead, you're embracing your innate nature.

Personal Growth: The journey of self-discovery is a path of continuous personal growth and self-improvement. You become more resilient, adaptable, and open to change.

Discovering your true essence is a profound and transformative journey of self-exploration. It involves peeling away the layers of external identities and societal conditioning to connect with your authentic self—the core of who you truly are. This journey leads to greater authenticity, purpose, inner peace, and meaningful relationships, ultimately enriching your life in profound ways.

Unveiling the Layers of Identity: Peeling Back the Complexities of Self

Identity is a multi-faceted and intricate concept, often compared to a layered tapestry woven from various threads of experiences, roles, beliefs, and influences. Unveiling the layers of identity is a profound journey of self-discovery, revealing the complexity and depth of who we are. It's a process that invites us to examine the intricacies of our self-perception, understand the forces that shape us, and ultimately, connect with our authentic selves.

The Multidimensionality of Identity:

Social Identity: The outermost layer of identity often consists of social roles and labels. These are the identities we acquire from society, such as our profession, ethnicity, nationality, gender, or religion. Social identity can be both a source of pride and a potential source of conformity or conflict.

Cultural Identity: Cultural identity encompasses the traditions, customs, values, and behaviors passed down through generations. It shapes our worldview, influences our sense of belonging, and informs how we relate to others. Cultural identity can be a source of rich heritage and diversity but can also lead to cultural clashes and identity crises.

Personal Identity: Beneath the surface layers of social and cultural identity lies our personal identity—the unique combination of traits, preferences, and experiences that make us who we are. It encompasses our interests, hobbies, passions, and the distinctive way we express ourselves.

Psychological Identity: Our psychological identity comprises our thoughts, beliefs, and emotions. It includes the narratives we create about ourselves, our self-concept, and our self-esteem. This layer often contains the stories we tell ourselves about our abilities, limitations, and worthiness.

Spiritual or Existential Identity: At the deepest layer of identity lies our spiritual or existential identity. This dimension pertains to our understanding of the larger questions of life, our connection to the universe, and our sense of purpose or meaning. It transcends the physical and material aspects of identity.

The Process of Unveiling Identity Layers:

Self-Reflection: To begin unveiling the layers of identity, engage in self-reflection. Take time to explore your thoughts, emotions, and beliefs. Consider your cultural and social influences and how they have shaped your identity.

Questioning Assumptions: Challenge assumptions and beliefs that you may have accepted without scrutiny. Ask yourself why you hold certain beliefs or values and whether they align with your true self. Question societal norms and expectations that may have influenced your identity.

Exploring Personal Interests: Dive into your personal interests and passions. Explore hobbies, activities, and pursuits that bring you joy and fulfillment. These activities can reveal deeper layers of your personal identity.

Seeking Diverse Perspectives: Expand your horizons by engaging with people from diverse backgrounds and perspectives. Exposure to different cultures and viewpoints can lead to a richer understanding of your own identity and the world around you.

Mindfulness and Self-Awareness: Practice mindfulness to connect with your inner self. Meditation and introspection can help you become more attuned to your thoughts, emotions, and beliefs, shedding light on the psychological layers of identity.

Challenges in Unveiling Identity Layers:

Fear of Uncertainty: Peeling back layers of identity can be unsettling because it may reveal aspects of ourselves we were previously unaware of or uncomfortable with. Embracing uncertainty and change is part of this process.

External Expectations: Society often imposes expectations based on external identities, which can create resistance to unveiling deeper layers. Overcoming societal pressures requires self-awareness and self-acceptance.

Vulnerability: Self-discovery often involves vulnerability, as it may entail confronting difficult emotions or acknowledging parts of ourselves we've suppressed. Embracing vulnerability is a crucial aspect of the process.

Benefits of Unveiling Identity Layers:

Authenticity: The journey of self-discovery leads to greater authenticity. You become more aligned with your true self and less influenced by external pressures.

Improved Self-Acceptance: Understanding the complexities of your identity fosters self-acceptance, including acceptance of your strengths and vulnerabilities.

Deeper Connections: As you unveil your authentic self, you can form deeper and more meaningful connections with others who appreciate and accept you for who you are.

Personal Growth: Self-discovery is a path of personal growth and self-improvement. It allows you to work on areas of your identity that you wish to develop.

Enhanced Well-Being: Ultimately, unveiling identity layers can lead to greater well-being, self-fulfillment, and a sense of purpose.

Unveiling the layers of identity is a profound and transformative journey that invites us to explore the complex tapestry of who we are. It involves self-reflection, questioning assumptions, and embracing vulnerability. By understanding the various dimensions of identity and aligning with our authentic selves, we can live more authentically, connect more deeply with others, and experience greater well-being and fulfilment.

The Ego and Its Influence: Understanding the Complex Interplay of Identity

The concept of the ego, deeply rooted in psychology and philosophy, has profound implications for understanding human behavior, self-perception, and interpersonal dynamics. The ego is a complex construct that influences our thoughts, emotions, and actions in multifaceted ways. To fully grasp its influence, we must delve into its nature, functions, and the effects it has on our lives.

Defining the Ego

The term "ego" has different meanings in various contexts, from psychology to philosophy and spirituality. In the realm of psychology, the ego is a fundamental component of Sigmund Freud's structural model of the mind. According to Freud, the mind is divided into three parts: the id (the primitive and instinctual part), the ego (the conscious and rational part), and the superego (the moral and societal part).

In this context, the ego is the mediator between the id and the superego, balancing our instinctual desires with societal norms and moral values. It strives to meet our needs and desires while conforming to the demands of the external world.

In a broader philosophical and spiritual sense, the ego is often associated with the sense of self or identity. It encompasses our self-concept, self-image, and the narratives we construct about ourselves. This aspect of the ego shapes our perception of who we are and how we relate to the world.

The Functions of the Ego:

Reality Testing: The ego's primary function is reality testing. It evaluates the external world and assesses the consequences of our actions. It helps us distinguish between fantasy and reality, ensuring that our behaviors align with the demands of our environment.

Defense Mechanisms: The ego employs defense mechanisms to protect the individual from distressing thoughts and emotions.

These mechanisms include denial, repression, projection, and rationalization. They serve as coping strategies to manage internal conflicts and maintain psychological equilibrium.

Identity Formation: The ego plays a central role in identity formation. It integrates our experiences, memories, and self-perceptions into a coherent sense of self. It shapes our self-concept and self-esteem, influencing how we view ourselves and present ourselves to others.

Decision-Making: The ego is involved in decision-making processes. It considers various options and evaluates their consequences based on both our desires and external factors. It helps us make choices that align with our goals and values.

The Influence of the Ego:

The ego's influence on human behavior and experience is pervasive and multifaceted. Here are several key aspects of its influence:

Self-Preservation: The ego's primary concern is self-preservation. It seeks to ensure our safety, comfort, and well-being. This drive for self-preservation can lead to behaviors such as seeking food, shelter, and security.

Desire and Gratification: The ego is closely tied to our desires and the pursuit of pleasure. It drives us to seek gratification for our needs and desires, whether they are physical, emotional, or psychological.

Identity and Self-Image: The ego shapes our identity and self-image. It influences how we perceive ourselves and present ourselves to others. It can lead to the development of self-concepts based on achievements, roles, or social status.

Conflict and Defense: Internal conflicts arise when the ego must balance competing desires, societal norms, and moral values. To cope with these conflicts, the ego employs defense mechanisms, which can have both adaptive and maladaptive effects on our mental health.

Interpersonal Relationships: The ego plays a crucial role in interpersonal relationships. It influences how we assert ourselves, negotiate conflicts, and seek validation from others. It can lead to behaviors driven by the need for recognition and affirmation.

Psychological Well-Being: The ego's influence extends to our psychological well-being. Excessive attachment to ego-driven desires or a rigid self-concept can contribute to emotional distress and dissatisfaction.

The Challenges and Pitfalls of the Ego:

While the ego serves important functions, it also presents challenges and potential pitfalls:

Ego-Centrism: Excessive ego-centrism can lead to self-centeredness and a lack of empathy for others. It can hinder our ability to consider the perspectives and needs of those around us.

Conflict and Rivalry: Ego-driven conflicts and rivalries can arise in various contexts, from personal relationships to competitive environments. These conflicts can be disruptive and detrimental to well-being.

Attachment to Identity: Strong attachment to a fixed self-identity can limit personal growth and adaptation. It can result in resistance to change and an aversion to challenges that threaten one's self-concept.

Defense Mechanisms: While defense mechanisms protect the ego from distress, they can also hinder self-awareness and prevent us from addressing underlying issues. Overreliance on defense mechanisms can lead to denial and avoidance.

Balancing the Ego:

Balancing the influence of the ego is a central aim in various psychological and spiritual traditions. Here are some approaches to achieving this balance:

Self-Reflection: Engaging in self-reflection and introspection allows individuals to gain insight into their ego-driven patterns and motivations. It promotes self-awareness and the capacity to make conscious choices.

Mindfulness: Mindfulness practices, such as meditation, cultivate awareness of the ego's influence on thoughts and emotions. They encourage non-judgmental observation and can help individuals detach from ego-driven reactions.

Self-Compassion: Practicing self-compassion involves treating oneself with kindness and understanding, even when facing ego-related challenges

Connecting with Your Authentic Self: Embracing Wholeness and Genuine Living

Connecting with your authentic self is a transformative journey that involves peeling away the layers of societal conditioning, external expectations, and self-imposed limitations to unveil the true essence of who you are. It's about embracing your uniqueness, aligning with your values, and living a life that reflects your genuine aspirations and desires. In this exploration, we delve into the significance of connecting with your authentic self, the process involved, and the profound benefits it brings.

The Significance of Connecting with Your Authentic Self:

Personal Fulfillment: When you connect with your authentic self, you align your life with your deepest values and passions. This alignment leads to a sense of fulfillment and contentment, as you are living in accordance with your true nature.

Self-Acceptance: Connecting with your authentic self involves accepting yourself fully, including your strengths, weaknesses, and quirks. This self-acceptance fosters greater self-esteem and resilience.

Improved Relationships: Authenticity in your interactions with others cultivates genuine connections. People are drawn to authenticity and are more likely to trust and connect with individuals who are true to themselves.

Clarity and Purpose: Understanding your authentic self provides clarity about your life's purpose and direction. You can set meaningful goals and make choices that resonate with your core values.

Emotional Well-Being: Living authentically reduces the internal conflicts and emotional stress that can arise from trying to conform to external expectations. It promotes emotional well-being and reduces anxiety and depression.

The Process of Connecting with Your Authentic Self:

Self-Reflection: Begin by setting aside time for self-reflection. Journaling, meditation, or contemplative walks can help you explore your thoughts, emotions, and values.

Questioning Assumptions: Challenge the assumptions and beliefs that have shaped your identity. Ask yourself why you hold certain beliefs or why you pursue specific goals. Consider whether they align with your authentic self.

Exploring Passions: Engage in activities and pursuits that genuinely excite you. Explore your interests and passions without the pressure of external expectations.

Cultivating Mindfulness: Mindfulness practices, such as meditation, can help you become more aware of your thoughts and emotions. They encourage non-judgmental observation, allowing you to detach from ego-driven reactions.

Seeking Authentic Relationships: Surround yourself with people who appreciate and support your authentic self. Authentic relationships provide a nurturing environment for your true self to flourish.

Challenges in Connecting with Your Authentic Self:

External Expectations: Society often imposes expectations and norms that can obscure your authentic self. Overcoming these external pressures requires self-awareness and the courage to be yourself.

Fear of Rejection: The fear of not being accepted or valued for who you truly are can be a significant barrier. It takes bravery to step into your authenticity, even when it means risking rejection.

Past Conditioning: Past experiences and conditioning can create beliefs and patterns that don't align with your authentic self. Overcoming these patterns may involve unraveling old conditioning and adopting new, more authentic beliefs.

The Benefits of Connecting with Your Authentic Self:

Authentic Living: Connecting with your authentic self allows you to live authentically, embracing who you are at your core without pretense or conformity.

Clarity and Purpose: Understanding your authentic self provides clarity and purpose in life. You can make choices and set goals that align with your true nature.

Improved Relationships: Authenticity fosters deeper and more meaningful connections with others. When you show up as your true self, you attract people who appreciate and accept you for who you are.

Inner Peace: Embracing your authentic self often leads to a sense of inner peace and contentment. You're no longer striving to be someone you're not but instead, you're embracing your innate nature.

Personal Growth: The journey of connecting with your authentic self is a path of continuous personal growth and self-improvement. You become more resilient, adaptable, and open to change.

The path to discovering your true self is a metamorphic voyage that beckons you to delve into the innermost recesses of your awareness with a receptive and open spirit. This route is one of genuine self-discovery, providing revelations about your innermost reflections, feelings, and the very essence of your being. As you traverse this path, you commit to an enduring quest of self-realization, acquiring deep understanding that sheds light on your journey towards self-improvement, overall wellness, and a life that is more genuine and interconnected.

The Inner Journey

The inner journey is a profound odyssey into the uncharted territories of your own psyche and soul. It's an expedition that takes you deep into the labyrinthine layers of your consciousness, unraveling the enigma of your true self. This voyage of self-discovery transcends the surface identities and societal masks we often wear, inviting you to uncover the essence of your being.

Understanding the Inner Journey:

Beyond the External Facade: The inner journey invites you to transcend the external facade you present to the world. It beckons you to peel away the veneer of social roles, titles, and expectations to reach the core of your authentic self.

Profound Self-Exploration: This odyssey is not a mere surface-level expedition but a profound exploration of your thoughts, emotions, beliefs, and values. It delves into the depths of your psyche, seeking to understand the intricacies of your inner world.

Connecting with Essence: At its core, the inner journey is about connecting with the essence of who you truly are. It's a process of self-revelation, a sacred unveiling of your genuine self that often lies obscured beneath layers of conditioning.

The Essence of the Inner Journey:

Soulful Self-Discovery: The inner journey is a quest to discover the soulful dimensions of your existence. It's a journey of self-exploration that transcends the physical and material, delving into the profound realms of consciousness and spirituality.

Revelation of Authenticity: As you traverse this inner landscape, you reveal the authenticity that resides within. You uncover your core values, beliefs, and aspirations, aligning your life with the truth of your being.

Awakening Inner Wisdom: The inner journey is a pilgrimage to awaken your inner wisdom. It calls you to listen to the whispers of your intuition and the profound insights that lie dormant within your soul.

Embarking on the Inner Odyssey:

Reflection and Contemplation: Commence the inner journey through reflection and contemplation. Take moments of stillness to explore your thoughts, emotions, and inner landscapes.

Questioning and Inquiry: Challenge the assumptions and beliefs that have shaped your identity. Engage in deep self-inquiry, asking profound questions about your values, purpose, and the nature of your existence.

Embracing Vulnerability: The inner journey often entails vulnerability. Embrace your vulnerabilities and imperfections as part of your unique tapestry. By doing so, you illuminate the path to your authentic self.

Seeking Inner Guidance: Cultivate mindfulness and introspection to connect with your inner guidance. Trust in the wisdom that resides within you and allow it to illuminate your path.

Challenges on the Inner Journey:

Fear of the Unknown: The uncharted territory of the inner journey can evoke fear of the unknown. Confronting these fears and stepping into uncertainty is an essential part of the process.

Resistance to Change: Your inner journey may challenge deeply ingrained patterns and beliefs. Resisting change is common, but embracing it allows for profound transformation.

Navigating Inner Turbulence: The inner journey can sometimes lead to inner turbulence as you confront suppressed emotions or conflicting beliefs. This turbulence, though challenging, is often a sign of growth and healing.

The Rewards of the Inner Journey:

Authentic Living: The inner journey leads to a life lived authentically. It liberates you from the shackles of conformity and empowers you to be your true self.

Clarity and Purpose: Understanding your authentic self provides clarity and purpose. It guides your choices and actions toward a life that aligns with your deepest values.

Fulfilling Relationships: Authenticity in your interactions fosters meaningful connections with others. Authentic relationships are built on genuine understanding and acceptance.

Inner Harmony: The inner journey often leads to a sense of inner harmony and contentment. It allows you to embrace the full spectrum of your being and find peace within.

In summary, the inner journey is a profound odyssey into the depths of self-exploration, a quest to unveil the essence of your true self. It transcends surface identities and societal expectations, inviting you to connect with the soulful dimensions of your existence. This journey of self-discovery leads to authenticity, clarity, and a profound sense of inner fulfillment, ultimately guiding you towards a life that is uniquely and authentically yours

Exploring Your Thoughts and Emotions: A Path to Self-Understanding and Growth

Exploring your thoughts and emotions is a crucial aspect of self-awareness and personal growth. It involves delving into the intricate landscape of your inner world to better understand your mental processes, feelings, and behaviors. In this exploration, we will uncover the benefits of such introspection, methods to engage in it, and how it can contribute to your overall well-being.

The Benefits of Exploring Your Thoughts and Emotions:

Self-Awareness: Delving into your thoughts and emotions deepens your self-awareness. You become more attuned to the patterns of your thinking, the triggers of your emotions, and how they influence your actions.

Emotional Regulation: Understanding your emotions allows you to regulate them more effectively. You can identify the root causes of negative emotions and develop strategies to manage them constructively.

Improved Decision-Making: Exploring your thoughts and emotions provides insights that can enhance decision-making. You can make choices that align with your values and long-term goals, rather than reacting impulsively.

Enhanced Relationships: Self-awareness gained from exploring your thoughts and emotions leads to better interpersonal relationships. You become more empathetic, understanding the perspectives and emotions of others more deeply.

Stress Reduction: Identifying and addressing sources of stress and anxiety through introspection can lead to reduced stress levels and increased overall well-being.

Methods for Exploring Your Thoughts and Emotions:

Journaling: Regularly journaling your thoughts and feelings is a powerful method of self-exploration. Write freely without judgment, allowing your thoughts to flow. Reviewing your journal over time can reveal patterns and insights.

Meditation: Mindfulness meditation involves observing your thoughts and emotions non-judgmentally. As you sit in quiet contemplation, notice the thoughts that arise and the emotions they trigger. This practice enhances self-awareness and emotional regulation.

Therapy and Counseling: Seeking the guidance of a therapist or counselor provides a structured space to explore your thoughts and emotions. Therapists use various techniques to help you gain insights and develop coping strategies.

Self-Questioning: Engage in self-questioning sessions where you ask yourself open-ended questions about your thoughts and emotions. For example, "What am I feeling right now, and why?" or "What thoughts are driving this emotion?"

Artistic Expression: Creative outlets such as writing, painting, or music can serve as a means of exploring your inner world. Artistic expression often allows for a deeper understanding of emotions that may be difficult to articulate verbally.

The Process of Exploring Your Thoughts and Emotions:

Create a Safe Space: Find a quiet and comfortable space where you can focus on your thoughts and emotions without distraction or interruption.

Observe Without Judgment: Approach your thoughts and emotions with curiosity and acceptance. Avoid labeling them as good or bad; instead, aim to understand them.

Mindful Awareness: Practice mindful awareness by observing your thoughts and emotions as they arise. Acknowledge them without attachment, allowing them to come and go like passing clouds.

Journaling: If you're journaling, write down your thoughts and emotions as they surface. Be honest and authentic in your expression.

Reflect: After engaging in introspection, take time to reflect on what you've discovered. Consider any patterns, triggers, or recurring themes in your thoughts and emotions.

Seek Support: If you encounter challenging emotions or thoughts that are difficult to navigate on your own, consider seeking support from a therapist, counselor, or support group.

Challenges in Exploring Your Thoughts and Emotions:

Avoidance: Some individuals may resist exploring their thoughts and emotions because it can bring up uncomfortable or painful feelings. However, avoidance often perpetuates emotional distress.

Over-Identification: On the other end of the spectrum, individuals may become overly identified with their thoughts and emotions, leading to rumination or emotional overwhelm. Striking a balance is essential.

Exploring your thoughts and emotions is a valuable journey of self-discovery and personal growth. It enhances self-awareness, emotional regulation, decision-making, and relationships. Utilizing methods such as journaling, meditation, therapy, and self-questioning allows you to navigate the intricate landscape of your inner world, leading to a deeper understanding of yourself and a more fulfilled and balanced life.

Navigating the Subconscious Mind: Unearthing the Depths of Your Inner World

The subconscious mind is a profound and enigmatic realm within our psyche, largely hidden from conscious awareness. Navigating this hidden territory can be a transformative journey, offering insights into our beliefs, behaviors, and emotions that often operate beneath the surface. In this exploration, we will delve into the significance of understanding the subconscious mind, the methods for doing so, and the potential benefits of this inner journey.

The Significance of Navigating the Subconscious Mind:

Uncovering Hidden Patterns: The subconscious mind is a repository of patterns, beliefs, and memories formed throughout our lives. By navigating it, we can uncover hidden patterns that influence our thoughts, emotions, and actions.

Self-Discovery: Exploring the subconscious allows us to gain a deeper understanding of ourselves. We can uncover suppressed emotions, unresolved conflicts, and aspects of our identity that may have been obscured.

Emotional Healing: Many emotional wounds and traumas reside in the subconscious. Navigating this realm can lead to emotional healing and the release of pent-up feelings, fostering greater emotional well-being.

Behavioral Transformation: Our subconscious beliefs often shape our behavior. By becoming aware of these beliefs, we can consciously choose to change behaviors that no longer serve us.

Enhanced Self-Awareness: Understanding the subconscious mind leads to enhanced self-awareness. We become attuned to the underlying motives and drivers of our actions, thoughts, and choices.

Methods for Navigating the Subconscious Mind:

Journaling: Regular journaling can provide insights into your subconscious. Write freely about your thoughts, dreams, and memories. Look for recurring themes and emotions.

Dream Analysis: Pay attention to your dreams, as they often contain symbols and themes that reflect your subconscious. Keeping a dream journal and analyzing your dreams can reveal hidden aspects of your mind.

Meditation: Meditation practices, particularly those focused on mindfulness and introspection, can help you access deeper layers of your consciousness. Mindful observation of thoughts and emotions can lead to insights.

Hypnotherapy: Hypnotherapy involves guided relaxation and focused attention to access the subconscious mind. A trained hypnotherapist can help you explore and work with the contents of your subconscious.

Therapeutic Techniques: Various therapeutic modalities, such as psychoanalysis and cognitive-behavioral therapy, can help you navigate the subconscious mind with the guidance of a trained therapist.

The Process of Navigating the Subconscious Mind:

Prepare for Exploration: Find a quiet and comfortable space where you can focus your attention inward. Set an intention to explore your subconscious mind.

Relaxation: Begin with a relaxation technique, such as deep breathing or progressive muscle relaxation, to quiet the conscious mind and open the gateway to the subconscious.

Mindful Observation: Whether through meditation, dream analysis, or another method, practice mindful observation of your thoughts, emotions, and memories as they surface. Avoid judgment and simply observe.

Record Insights: Keep a journal to record any insights, memories, or patterns that emerge during your exploration. Document your experiences without filtering or censorship.

Seek Professional Guidance: If you encounter deep-seated traumas or emotional challenges during your exploration, consider seeking the guidance of a trained therapist or counselor.

Challenges in Navigating the Subconscious Mind:

Resistance: The subconscious mind may resist exploration, especially if it harbors painful memories or unresolved emotions. Resistance is natural but can be overcome with patience and persistence.

Overwhelming Emotions: Exploring the subconscious may bring up intense emotions. It's essential to have healthy coping mechanisms and support systems in place to manage these emotions effectively.

Benefits of Navigating the Subconscious Mind:

Emotional Healing: Exploring the subconscious can lead to the healing of deep emotional wounds and the release of long-held emotional burdens.

Behavioral Transformation: Understanding subconscious beliefs and patterns empowers you to make conscious choices and change behaviors that no longer serve your well-being.

Enhanced Self-Awareness: Navigating the subconscious enhances self-awareness, providing a deeper understanding of your motivations, fears, and desires.

Personal Growth: The insights gained from exploring the subconscious can lead to personal growth, self-acceptance, and a greater sense of inner peace.

Resolution of Inner Conflicts: By addressing subconscious conflicts and contradictions, you can resolve inner turmoil and experience greater harmony within yourself.

Navigating the subconscious mind is a profound journey of self-discovery and healing. It offers the potential for profound insights, emotional release, and personal transformation. By engaging in methods such as journaling, dream analysis, meditation, or therapy, you can access the hidden depths of your psyche, gaining a deeper understanding of yourself and ultimately achieving greater emotional well-being and personal growth.

Insights from Meditation, Self-Reflection, and Journaling: Nurturing Self-Awareness and Inner Growth

Meditation, self-reflection, and journaling are powerful tools for delving into the recesses of your consciousness, unearthing profound insights, and fostering self-awareness. This trifecta of practices empowers you to connect with your inner self, navigate your thoughts and emotions, and chart a path of personal growth. In this exploration, we will delve into the significance of these practices, their methods, and the rich insights they can bring.

The Significance of Meditation, Self-Reflection, and Journaling:

Enhanced Self-Awareness: These practices provide a mirror to your inner world, allowing you to observe your thoughts, emotions, and behaviors with clarity. This heightened self-awareness is the cornerstone of personal growth.

Emotional Regulation: By regularly engaging in these practices, you develop the ability to recognize and regulate your emotions. You can navigate the ebb and flow of your inner landscape with greater ease.

Clarity of Thought: Meditation, self-reflection, and journaling help declutter your mind, fostering clarity of thought. This clarity empowers you to make informed decisions and solve problems more effectively.

Stress Reduction: These practices offer effective tools for managing stress and anxiety. They encourage relaxation, grounding, and the release of emotional tension.

Methods for Meditation, Self-Reflection, and Journaling:

Meditation:

Mindfulness Meditation: Sit in a quiet space, focus on your breath, and observe your thoughts and sensations as they arise without judgment. Bring your attention back to your breath when it wanders.

Guided Meditation: Follow guided meditation sessions that lead you through visualization or specific mindfulness exercises, helping you explore different aspects of your consciousness.

Self-Reflection:

Set Aside Time: Dedicate regular periods for self-reflection, whether daily or weekly. Create a quiet, undisturbed space to facilitate deep introspection.

Ask Open-Ended Questions: Pose open-ended questions to yourself, such as "What am I feeling right now, and why?" or "What are my core values, and how do they align with my life choices?"

Contemplative Practices: Engage in practices like mindfulness walks, where you consciously observe your surroundings and your inner state, fostering self-awareness.

Journaling:

Stream of Consciousness: Write without inhibition, allowing your thoughts and feelings to flow freely onto the pages. Don't censor or judge; simply record your inner world.

Focused Journaling: Create journals with specific themes, such as a gratitude journal, a dream journal, or a journal dedicated to self-reflection and personal growth.

Regular Practice: Establish a consistent journaling routine, whether it's daily, weekly, or whenever insights and reflections arise. Review your journal periodically to track your growth.

The Process and Benefits of Insights from Meditation, Self-Reflection, and Journaling:

Observation and Awareness:

Through meditation, you observe your thoughts and emotions as they arise, cultivating awareness of your mental landscape.

Self-reflection invites you to ponder life's complexities, prompting you to explore your values, beliefs, and motivations.

Journaling captures your inner dialogue, serving as a record of your evolving thoughts, emotions, and insights.

Insight and Revelation:

Over time, these practices offer profound insights into your thought patterns, emotional triggers, and the underlying causes of your behaviors.

You may uncover recurring themes, unresolved conflicts, or limiting beliefs that have influenced your decisions and actions.

Integration and Growth:

Armed with these insights, you can consciously choose to integrate positive changes into your life. You may revise your goals, make informed decisions, and develop healthier coping strategies.

Personal growth becomes a natural byproduct of this process, as you shed light on your inner world and evolve in alignment with your authentic self.

Stress Reduction and Emotional Well-Being:

Meditation, self-reflection, and journaling serve as effective tools for managing stress and enhancing emotional well-being. They promote relaxation, emotional processing, and resilience.

By recognizing and addressing sources of stress and anxiety, you can experience a greater sense of inner peace and balance.

Challenges in Insights from Meditation, Self-Reflection, and Journaling:

Consistency: Maintaining a regular practice can be challenging. Finding the time and discipline to engage in these activities may require effort.

Resistance: The exploration of your inner world may evoke resistance or discomfort, particularly when confronting deep-seated emotions or challenging beliefs.

Overthinking: While introspection is valuable, overanalyzing and rumination can lead to a cycle of negative thought patterns. Striking a balance is essential.

In conclusion, the triumvirate of meditation, self-reflection, and journaling is a powerful means of nurturing self-awareness and fostering personal growth. By embracing these practices, you embark on a journey of inner exploration, uncovering profound insights, and forging a path of self-discovery and emotional well-being. These tools empower you to navigate the complexities of your inner world, making conscious choices that align with your authentic self and leading to a more fulfilling and harmonious life.

Spirituality and Meditation

Spirituality and meditation are intertwined practices that invite individuals to embark on a profound journey of inner exploration, self-discovery, and connection with the divine or transcendent. This harmonious union offers a pathway to inner peace, self-realization, and a deeper understanding of the interconnectedness of all existence. In this exploration, we will delve into the significance of spirituality and meditation, their relationship, and the transformative benefits they bestow.

The Significance of Spirituality and Meditation:

Inner Exploration: Spirituality and meditation encourage individuals to venture inward, exploring the depths of their consciousness and uncovering the truths of their existence. This inner journey leads to self-discovery and self-realization.

Transcendence: Both practices seek to transcend the confines of the ego and the material world. They aim to connect with higher states of consciousness, divine realms, or a universal source of wisdom and love.

Connection: Spirituality and meditation foster a profound sense of connection, not only with the self but with all living beings and the cosmos. They emphasize the interconnectedness of existence.

Peace and Well-Being: These practices offer a sanctuary of inner peace, reducing stress, anxiety, and suffering. They promote emotional balance and a heightened sense of well-being.

Purpose and Meaning: Spirituality and meditation often lead individuals to explore their life's purpose and seek greater meaning in their existence. They provide a framework for aligning one's actions with their deepest values.

The Relationship Between Spirituality and Meditation:

Meditative Practices: Meditation is a core component of spiritual traditions worldwide. It serves as a means to quiet the mind, open the heart, and create a receptive state for spiritual experiences.

Deepening Spirituality: Meditation deepens one's spiritual connection by facilitating direct experiences of the divine, transcendental, or sacred. It allows individuals to access higher states of consciousness beyond ordinary perception.

Inner Transformation: Both spirituality and meditation aim at inner transformation. They invite individuals to transcend the ego, cultivate virtues like compassion and love, and expand their awareness of reality.

Meditative Techniques in Spirituality:

Mindfulness Meditation: Rooted in Buddhist traditions, mindfulness meditation encourages present-moment awareness, promoting deep insight and inner peace.

Loving-Kindness Meditation (Metta): This practice emanates love and compassion towards oneself and others, fostering a sense of interconnectedness and empathy.

Transcendental Meditation (TM): TM is a specific mantra-based meditation technique that aims to access a state of pure consciousness and inner bliss.

Chakra Meditation: Derived from Hindu and yogic traditions, chakra meditation focuses on balancing and energizing the body's energy centers (chakras) to harmonize the mind, body, and spirit.

Guided Visualization: Often used in New Age and spiritual practices, guided visualization takes individuals on mental journeys to connect with their inner wisdom or divine realms.

The Benefits of the Union of Spirituality and Meditation:

Spiritual Growth: This union nurtures spiritual growth by deepening one's connection with the divine or the universe. It provides a framework for exploring existential questions and finding profound answers.

Inner Peace: Spirituality and meditation offer a sanctuary of inner peace, helping individuals find serenity amid life's challenges and uncertainties.

Compassion and Empathy: Meditation, when integrated with spirituality, fosters qualities like compassion, love, and empathy, enhancing relationships and fostering a sense of unity with all living beings.

Purpose and Fulfillment: The combination of spirituality and meditation often leads individuals to discover their life's purpose and experience a sense of fulfillment by aligning with their higher calling.

Enhanced Well-Being: This union promotes emotional well-being, reducing stress, anxiety, and depression. It cultivates a positive outlook on life and the ability to navigate adversity with resilience.

Challenges in the Practice of Spirituality and Meditation:

Doubt and Skepticism: Some individuals may approach spirituality and meditation with skepticism. Overcoming doubt and cultivating faith in the process can be a challenge.

Distractions: In our fast-paced world, finding the time and space for consistent meditation and spiritual practice can be challenging.

Ego Obstacles: The ego often resists dissolution, and individuals may encounter resistance when attempting to transcend the self-centered mind.

Spirituality and meditation together create a harmonious and transformative journey into the depths of human consciousness and the realm of the divine or transcendent. They offer a pathway to inner peace, self-realization, and a profound understanding of the interconnectedness of all existence. By embracing the union of spirituality and meditation, individuals can embark on a sacred odyssey that nurtures their spiritual growth, fosters compassion, and leads to a life filled with purpose, meaning, and well-being

The Intersection of Meditation and Spirituality: A Journey into the Sacred Self

The intersection of meditation and spirituality forms a profound crossroads where inner exploration, self-discovery, and connection with the divine converge. It is a sacred space where individuals embark on a transformative journey of awakening, seeking to understand their true nature, find meaning in life, and establish a deep connection with the spiritual dimension. In this exploration, we will delve into the significance of this intersection, its methods, and the transformative impact it can have on one's life.

The Significance of the Intersection of Meditation and Spirituality:

Awakening to the Self: At this intersection, individuals awaken to their true selves, transcending the limited identity of the ego. They connect with the core of their being, often described as the soul or spirit.

Connection with the Divine: Meditation and spirituality converge to facilitate a profound connection with the divine, the universal consciousness, or a higher power. This connection brings a sense of reverence and devotion to one's life.

Transcending Ego: Both meditation and spirituality challenge the dominance of the ego, which is often driven by worldly desires and attachments. This transcendence allows individuals to experience a sense of liberation and inner peace.

Self-Realization: The intersection encourages self-realization, where individuals come to understand their intrinsic worth, purpose, and the interconnectedness of all existence.

Methods at the Intersection of Meditation and Spirituality:

Contemplative Meditation: Contemplative practices involve reflecting on sacred texts, teachings, or questions related to the nature of existence. This allows individuals to delve deeply into spiritual wisdom.

Transcendental Meditation (TM): TM is a specific mantra-based meditation technique that aims to transcend ordinary thought and connect with the transcendental, often described as the source of all being.

Chakra Meditation: Rooted in yoga and Eastern spirituality, chakra meditation focuses on aligning and balancing the body's energy centers (chakras) to promote spiritual growth and harmony.

Mystical Meditation: Mystical meditation seeks to induce mystical or transcendent experiences, connecting individuals with the divine or the ineffable through deep contemplation and surrender.

Mindfulness Meditation: While often associated with secular practices, mindfulness can be deeply spiritual when used as a means to connect with the present moment and cultivate self-awareness.

The Transformative Impact at the Intersection:

Spiritual Awakening: The intersection of meditation and spirituality often leads to spiritual awakening, where individuals experience profound shifts in consciousness and an expanded sense of self.

Deep Inner Peace: This convergence fosters inner peace that is not dependent on external circumstances. Individuals become more resilient in the face of life's challenges.

Compassion and Empathy: The connection with the divine and the recognition of the interconnectedness of all existence often cultivate qualities like compassion, love, and empathy for others.

Purpose and Meaning: Through meditation and spirituality, individuals often discover a deeper sense of purpose and meaning in life. They align their actions with their spiritual values.

Surrender and Acceptance: The intersection encourages surrendering to the flow of life and accepting things as they are, leading to a sense of trust and serenity.

Challenges at the Intersection:

Doubt and Skepticism: Individuals may initially approach spiritual practices with doubt or skepticism. Overcoming these barriers often requires patience and exploration.

Ego Resistance: The ego often resists surrender and dissolution. Facing this resistance can be a challenging aspect of the journey.

Time and Commitment: Consistent meditation and spiritual practice require time and commitment, which can be difficult to maintain in the busyness of modern life.

In Conclusion:

The intersection of meditation and spirituality is a sacred juncture where individuals embark on a profound journey of self-discovery, connection with the divine, and inner transformation. It offers the opportunity to transcend the ego, find inner peace, and discover a deeper purpose in life. By embracing this intersection, individuals can embark on a spiritual odyssey that leads to a more profound and meaningful existence, fostering a sense of interconnectedness and reverence for all of creation.

Transcendent Experiences in Meditation: Journeying Beyond the Self

Transcendent experiences in meditation are profound and mystical moments where individuals go beyond their ordinary sense of self and connect with a higher, transcendent reality. These experiences are often described as moments of pure consciousness, unity with the universe, or encounters with the divine. In this exploration, we will delve into the significance of transcendent experiences, their characteristics, and the transformative impact they can have on one's life.

The Significance of Transcendent Experiences in Meditation:

Awakening to the Infinite: Transcendent experiences in meditation awaken individuals to the infinite nature of consciousness. They provide glimpses into the boundless and timeless reality that transcends the limitations of the ego.

Connection with the Divine: Many individuals describe these experiences as moments of direct connection with the divine, the sacred, or a universal source of wisdom and love. They foster a sense of reverence and devotion.

Transcending Ego: Transcendent experiences often involve a temporary dissolution of the ego—the sense of a separate self. This dissolution leads to a deep sense of oneness and interconnectedness with all existence.

Profound Inner Peace: These experiences bring a profound sense of inner peace and serenity that is not dependent on external circumstances. They often lead to a lasting reduction in anxiety and stress.

Spiritual Growth: Transcendent experiences can be catalysts for spiritual growth, prompting individuals to explore deeper questions about the nature of reality, purpose in life, and the interconnectedness of all beings.

Characteristics of Transcendent Experiences in Meditation:

Loss of Self: During a transcendent experience, individuals often report a loss of the sense of self. They may no longer feel like a separate individual but rather part of a larger, unified consciousness.

Timelessness: Time often seems to stand still or lose its significance during these moments. Past and future dissolve, leaving only the present moment.

Intense Bliss: A profound sense of bliss, ecstasy, or joy is a common characteristic of transcendent experiences. This bliss is often described as pure and unconditional.

Unity and Interconnectedness: Individuals frequently report feeling deeply connected with all living beings and the entire universe. They experience a sense of unity that transcends physical boundaries.

Ineffability: Transcendent experiences are often challenging to describe in words. They are ineffable, beyond the capacity of language to fully capture.

The Transformative Impact of Transcendent Experiences:

Shift in Consciousness: These experiences bring about a shift in consciousness, expanding one's understanding of reality and the self. They often lead to a more open and inclusive worldview.

Deep Inner Peace: The profound peace experienced during these moments can have a lasting impact, reducing stress, anxiety, and promoting emotional well-being.

Spiritual Growth: Transcendent experiences often catalyze spiritual growth, prompting individuals to explore their spirituality, seek purpose in life, and cultivate qualities like compassion and empathy.

Enhanced Resilience: Individuals who have experienced transcendent moments often exhibit enhanced resilience in the face of life's challenges. They possess a sense of trust and surrender to the flow of life.

Challenges in Experiencing Transcendent Moments:

Inconsistency: Transcendent experiences are often spontaneous and unpredictable. Individuals may struggle to reproduce them at will.

Integration: Integrating these experiences into daily life can be challenging. Individuals may grapple with how to bring the insights and wisdom gained from such moments into their everyday existence.

Doubt and Skepticism: Some individuals may doubt the authenticity or significance of their transcendent experiences, particularly if they do not align with their existing belief systems.

Transcendent experiences in meditation are rare and mystical moments where individuals transcend their ordinary sense of self and connect with a higher, transcendent reality. These experiences have the potential to profoundly transform one's understanding of consciousness, the self, and the universe. They bring a deep sense of inner peace, interconnectedness, and spiritual growth. While they may be elusive and challenging to describe, their impact can be life-altering, fostering a sense of unity, purpose, and reverence for the mysteries of existence.

Connecting with Your Higher Self: A Journey to Inner Wisdom and Guidance

Connecting with your higher self is a transformative and profound inner journey that involves accessing a deeper level of consciousness and wisdom within yourself. This higher self is often described as the inner voice of intuition, the repository of inner guidance, and the source of your authentic wisdom. In this exploration, we will delve into the significance of connecting with your higher self, the methods to do so, and the life-changing benefits it can bring.

The Significance of Connecting with Your Higher Self:

Inner Wisdom: Your higher self is a reservoir of inner wisdom and insight. By connecting with it, you gain access to a wellspring of knowledge and guidance that can help you navigate life's challenges and make informed decisions.

Authenticity: The higher self represents your true, authentic self—free from ego-driven desires, fears, and external influences. Connecting with it allows you to live in alignment with your core values and purpose.

Intuition and Clarity: The connection with your higher self sharpens your intuition and provides clarity in decision-making. You become attuned to your inner compass, helping you discern the right path in life.

Emotional Resilience: Accessing your higher self can enhance emotional resilience and inner peace. It empowers you to manage stress, anxiety, and negative emotions with greater ease.

Spiritual Growth: This connection often leads to spiritual growth and self-realization, fostering a sense of unity with all existence and a deeper understanding of the nature of reality.

Methods for Connecting with Your Higher Self:

Meditation: Regular meditation, particularly mindfulness or introspective practices, creates a receptive state for connecting with your higher self. During meditation, you can quiet the chatter of the ego and listen to your inner guidance.

Journaling: Journaling can be a powerful tool for connecting with your higher self. Write down your thoughts, feelings, and inner dialogues. Ask open-ended questions and wait for intuitive responses to flow onto the pages.

Mindful Awareness: Engage in daily activities with mindful awareness. Pay attention to your thoughts, feelings, and sensations as you go about your day. This heightened awareness can help you discern the voice of your higher self.

Nature and Solitude: Spend time in nature and seek solitude to connect with your higher self. These settings often facilitate a sense of inner peace and clarity, making it easier to access your intuition.

Visualization: Use guided visualization techniques to imagine a dialogue or meeting with your higher self. Visualize asking questions and receiving guidance.

The Process of Connecting with Your Higher Self:

Set Intentions: Begin your practice with a clear intention to connect with your higher self. State your desire for guidance, wisdom, and clarity.

Quiet the Mind: Through meditation or mindfulness, quiet the mental chatter and ego-driven thoughts. Create a still, receptive space within yourself.

Ask Questions: Pose questions or seek guidance from your higher self. These questions can relate to life decisions, personal growth, or any aspect of your life.

Listen and Feel: Pay attention to any intuitive thoughts, feelings, or sensations that arise. Your higher self may communicate through a sense of knowing, a gentle voice, or a feeling of peace.

Trust and Acceptance: Trust in the process and accept the guidance that comes. Even if it doesn't match your ego's expectations, be open to receiving insights from your higher self.

Benefits of Connecting with Your Higher Self:

Inner Guidance: Connecting with your higher self provides you with a reliable source of inner guidance and wisdom for navigating life's challenges.

Authentic Living: It empowers you to live authentically, aligning your actions with your core values and purpose.

Emotional Well-Being: Accessing your higher self can lead to emotional resilience, inner peace, and reduced stress.

Clarity and Intuition: You gain clarity in decision-making and sharpened intuition, helping you make choices that align with your true self.

Spiritual Growth: This connection often leads to spiritual growth, fostering a sense of interconnectedness and unity with the universe.

Challenges in Connecting with Your Higher Self:

Doubt and Impatience: Doubt and impatience can hinder the process. It's important to trust and allow the connection to unfold naturally.

Ego Interference: The ego may resist the connection, as it often operates from a place of fear and control. Recognize and transcend ego-driven thoughts and desires.

Distractions: The busyness of daily life and external distractions can make it challenging to create the inner stillness needed to connect with your higher self.

Connecting with your higher self is a sacred journey of self-discovery, inner guidance, and personal transformation. It provides access to a wellspring of wisdom, intuition, and authenticity within yourself. By embracing this connection, you can navigate life with greater clarity, purpose, and emotional well-being, ultimately leading to a deeper understanding of your true self and the nature of existence.

Meditation and Intuition

Meditation and intuition are deeply intertwined practices that empower individuals to tap into their inner wisdom and navigate life's complexities with clarity and insight. Meditation serves as a vehicle for quieting the mind and creating a receptive space, while intuition acts as a guide, offering subtle yet profound wisdom and guidance. In this exploration, we will delve into the significance of meditation and intuition, their relationship, and how they collectively enhance personal growth and decision-making.

The Significance of Meditation and Intuition:

Inner Wisdom: Meditation and intuition provide a pathway to access your inner wisdom—the deep reservoir of knowledge and understanding that exists within you. This inner wisdom often transcends conventional logic and reasoning.

Clarity and Insight: Meditation helps clear the clutter of everyday thoughts, creating mental clarity. Intuition then fills this space with insights, allowing you to perceive hidden truths and make informed decisions.

Trust in Inner Knowing: Cultivating intuition through meditation fosters trust in your inner knowing. This trust enables you to rely on your instincts and gut feelings, especially in situations where concrete evidence is lacking.

Alignment with Authentic Self: Both practices guide you toward alignment with your authentic self, helping you make choices and live in ways that are congruent with your values, purpose, and inner essence.

Problem Solving: Intuition often serves as a valuable problem-solving tool, providing creative solutions and innovative ideas that may not be evident through analytical thinking alone.

The Relationship Between Meditation and Intuition:

Preparation for Intuition: Meditation prepares the mind to receive intuitive insights by calming mental chatter and reducing the influence of ego-driven thoughts. It creates the receptive space necessary for intuition to flourish.

Heightened Awareness: Meditation heightens awareness, making individuals more attuned to subtle sensations, emotions, and intuitive nudges. This heightened awareness allows for a more accurate reception of intuitive information.

Clarity and Discernment: Meditation sharpens mental clarity and discernment, which are essential for interpreting intuitive insights accurately. It enables individuals to distinguish between true intuition and mere wishful thinking or fear-based reactions.

Cultivating Intuition through Meditation:

Regular Practice: Consistent meditation practice is essential for cultivating intuition. Set aside dedicated time each day to meditate, creating a habit that nurtures inner stillness and receptivity.

Mindfulness Meditation: Mindfulness meditation, which involves non-judgmental awareness of the present moment, is particularly conducive to cultivating intuition. It helps you become more attuned to your inner landscape.

Open-Ended Questions: During meditation, pose open-ended questions or present a particular issue or dilemma to your mind. Allow these questions to percolate in your consciousness, trusting that intuitive insights may arise.

Silent Observation: Practice silent observation during meditation. Instead of actively seeking answers, observe your thoughts, feelings, and sensations. Be open to whatever arises.

Intuitive Journaling: After meditation sessions, journal your experiences and any intuitive insights or hunches that emerged.

Over time, you may notice patterns or recurring themes in your intuitive guidance.

Benefits of Combining Meditation and Intuition:

Enhanced Decision-Making: The marriage of meditation and intuition leads to more informed and intuitive decision-making. You can navigate complex choices with greater confidence.

Creative Inspiration: Intuition often fuels creativity. Meditation provides the mental space for creative inspiration to blossom, leading to innovative ideas and solutions.

Stress Reduction: Meditation reduces stress, while intuition can guide you in managing challenging situations calmly and effectively.

Personal Growth: The integration of meditation and intuition supports personal growth, encouraging alignment with your authentic self and fostering a deeper understanding of your inner world.

Emotional Well-Being: These practices contribute to emotional well-being by reducing anxiety, enhancing emotional resilience, and promoting inner peace.

Challenges in Cultivating Intuition through Meditation:

Impatience: Developing intuition through meditation requires patience. Intuitive insights may not come instantly but tend to evolve gradually.

Doubt: Doubt in the authenticity of intuitive insights can hinder the process. Cultivating trust in your inner guidance is an essential aspect of this journey.

Distraction: External distractions and a busy lifestyle can disrupt the consistency of meditation practice, making it challenging to connect with intuition.

The synergy between meditation and intuition offers a profound avenue for accessing inner wisdom and enhancing decision-making. Through meditation, you create the mental space for intuition to flourish, while intuition enriches your meditation practice with insights that transcend conventional thinking. Together, these practices empower you to navigate life with clarity, authenticity, and a deep sense of inner knowing, ultimately leading to personal growth and emotional well-being.

Developing Intuitive Abilities through Meditation: Unleashing Inner Insight

Developing intuitive abilities through meditation is a transformative journey that empowers individuals to tap into their innate capacity for insight, foresight, and inner knowing. Intuition, often referred to as the "sixth sense," offers a profound source of guidance and wisdom that transcends rational thought. When combined with meditation, it becomes a powerful tool for navigating life's complexities with clarity and authenticity. In this exploration, we will delve into the significance of developing intuitive abilities, methods to do so, and the life-changing benefits it can bring.

The Significance of Developing Intuitive Abilities:

Inner Guidance: Developing intuitive abilities grants access to a wellspring of inner guidance. It serves as a compass, helping individuals make informed decisions and navigate life's challenges with greater ease.

Clarity and Insight: Intuition provides clarity and insight beyond the limitations of logical reasoning. It enables individuals to perceive hidden truths, make creative connections, and find innovative solutions to problems.

Trust in Inner Knowing: As intuitive abilities are honed, trust in one's inner knowing deepens. This trust empowers individuals to rely on their instincts and gut feelings, especially in situations where concrete evidence is scarce.

Alignment with Authentic Self: Developing intuition often leads to greater alignment with one's authentic self. It helps individuals make choices and live in ways that resonate with their core values and purpose.

Enhanced Decision-Making: The intuitive mind complements rational thinking by providing additional information and perspectives. This enhances decision-making, particularly in situations that require a holistic understanding.

Methods for Developing Intuitive Abilities through Meditation:

Mindfulness Meditation: Regular mindfulness meditation cultivates present-moment awareness. It sharpens the intuitive senses by helping individuals attune to subtle sensations, emotions, and intuitive nudges.

Silent Observation: During meditation, practice silent observation. Instead of actively seeking answers, observe your thoughts, feelings, and sensations. Be open to intuitive insights that may arise.

Intuitive Visualization: Use guided visualization techniques to imagine a scenario where you seek intuitive guidance. Visualize the situation and invite intuitive insights to surface during your meditation.

Intuitive Journaling: After meditation sessions, journal your experiences and any intuitive insights or hunches that emerged. Over time, you may notice patterns or recurring themes in your intuitive guidance.

Chakra Meditation: Chakra meditation focuses on balancing and aligning the body's energy centers (chakras). A balanced energy system can enhance intuitive abilities by creating harmony within the mind and body.

The Process of Developing Intuitive Abilities:

Set Intentions: Begin your meditation practice with a clear intention to develop your intuitive abilities. State your desire for greater insight, guidance, and trust in your intuition.

Quiet the Mind: Meditation is the foundation for developing intuition. It quiets the mental chatter, creating a receptive space for intuitive insights to emerge.

Ask Intuitive Questions: During meditation, pose questions or present specific situations that you seek intuitive guidance on. Allow these questions to permeate your consciousness, trusting that intuitive answers may arise.

Listen and Feel: Pay attention to any intuitive thoughts, feelings, or sensations that arise during or after meditation. Your intuition may communicate through a sense of knowing, a gentle inner voice, or a feeling of resonance.

Trust and Acceptance: Trust in the process and accept the guidance that comes. Even if intuitive insights do not align with your ego's expectations, be open to receiving and exploring them.

Benefits of Developing Intuitive Abilities:

Enhanced Decision-Making: Developing intuitive abilities enriches decision-making by providing additional insights and perspectives. It helps individuals make choices aligned with their true selves.

Creative Problem Solving: Intuition often sparks creativity and innovative thinking. It assists in finding novel solutions to challenges and encourages thinking outside the box.

Emotional Resilience: A well-developed intuition can enhance emotional resilience. It empowers individuals to manage stress, anxiety, and difficult emotions with greater ease.

Alignment with Authenticity: Developing intuition fosters alignment with one's authentic self and core values. It encourages living a life that resonates with one's deepest desires and purpose.

Deep Inner Trust: As intuitive abilities grow, individuals cultivate a deep inner trust in their own insights and decisions, even when they appear unconventional or contrary to external advice.

Challenges in Developing Intuitive Abilities through Meditation:

Impatience: Developing intuition is a gradual process. Impatience can hinder progress. It's essential to be patient and allow the intuitive senses to develop naturally.

Doubt: Doubt in the authenticity of intuitive insights can be a stumbling block. Cultivating trust in your inner guidance is crucial for nurturing intuition.

Distraction: External distractions and a busy lifestyle may disrupt meditation practice, making it challenging to connect with intuitive abilities consistently.

Developing intuitive abilities through meditation is a profound journey of self-discovery, inner guidance, and personal transformation. It provides access to a wellspring of insight, creativity, and authentic living. By embracing this path, individuals can navigate life with greater clarity, trust in their inner wisdom, and a profound sense of alignment with their true selves, ultimately leading to personal growth and emotional well-being

Trusting your inner wisdom is a concept rooted in self-awareness, intuition, and self-trust. It involves relying on your inner guidance, instincts, and knowledge to make decisions and navigate life's challenges. Here's an elaborate explanation of this important idea:

Self-awareness: Trusting your inner wisdom begins with understanding yourself on a deep level. This means recognizing your values, beliefs, strengths, weaknesses, and past experiences. Self-awareness enables you to tap into your inner wisdom because it allows you to identify patterns in your thoughts, feelings, and behaviors.

Intuition: Intuition is often described as a gut feeling or an inner knowing. It's that sense you have about something without being able to explain it logically. Trusting your inner wisdom involves listening to your intuition and considering it as a valuable source of information. Intuition can be especially helpful in situations where you don't have all the facts or when making decisions based solely on data feels insufficient.

Inner guidance: Your inner wisdom can act as a guide in your life. It's that voice inside you that offers insights, suggestions, and even warnings. It can help you navigate complex situations, make choices aligned with your values, and provide a sense of direction. Trusting your inner guidance means giving it the space to speak and actively listening to it.

Learning from experience: Your inner wisdom is often informed by your life experiences. It's the accumulation of knowledge and wisdom gained from past successes and failures. Trusting your inner wisdom means acknowledging that you have the capacity to learn from your mistakes and apply those lessons to future decisions.

Self-trust: Trusting your inner wisdom requires a level of self-trust. You must believe in your ability to make sound judgments and choices. This doesn't mean you'll always be right or that you won't make mistakes, but it means having confidence in your ability to learn and grow from those experiences.

Balancing intuition and logic: While trusting your inner wisdom is important, it doesn't mean disregarding logic and reason. It's about finding a balance between your intuitive insights and rational thinking. Sometimes, these two aspects of decision-making can complement each other, leading to more well-rounded choices.

Meditation and mindfulness: Practices like meditation and mindfulness can help you connect with your inner wisdom. These techniques encourage you to quiet your mind, listen to your inner voice, and become more attuned to your thoughts and feelings.

Seeking input when needed: Trusting your inner wisdom doesn't mean you should always rely solely on yourself. It's essential to recognize when a situation requires external input, advice, or expertise. Trusting your inner wisdom can also involve knowing when to seek help or collaborate with others.

Personal growth and development: As you grow and develop as an individual, your inner wisdom can become more refined and reliable. Engaging in personal growth activities such as reading, learning, and reflecting on your experiences can enhance your inner wisdom.

In summary, trusting your inner wisdom is about recognizing the valuable insights and guidance within yourself. It involves self-awareness, intuition, and the ability to make decisions based on a combination of your inner guidance and rational thinking. By developing and trusting your inner wisdom, you can make choices that are more authentic, aligned with your values, and ultimately lead to a more fulfilling life.

Meditation can be a powerful tool for enhancing your intuition by helping you connect with your inner self and quieting the noise of the external world. Here are some meditation practices that can specifically promote intuition:

Mindful Meditation:

Find a quiet and comfortable place to sit or lie down.

Close your eyes and take a few deep breaths to center yourself.

Focus your attention on your breath. Notice the sensation of each inhale and exhale.

When your mind starts to wander, gently bring your focus back to your breath.

As you continue this practice, you may start to notice subtle thoughts, feelings, or insights emerging. Pay attention to them without judgment.

Body Scan Meditation:

Begin in a comfortable position, either sitting or lying down.

Close your eyes and take a few deep breaths.

Start at the top of your head and slowly move your attention down through your body, paying attention to any sensations or tension you might feel.

As you focus on each body part, listen to what your body is telling you. It may reveal insights or sensations related to your intuition.

Visualization Meditation:

Sit comfortably and close your eyes.

Imagine a peaceful and safe place, like a forest, beach, or meadow.

In this visualization, let your intuition guide you. Allow any images, feelings, or insights to arise naturally.

Trust your intuition to lead you through this mental landscape and provide insights or answers to questions you may have.

Journaling Meditation:

Begin by sitting in a quiet space with a journal or notebook and a pen.

Start with some deep breaths to center yourself.

Write down a question or issue you'd like insights on.

Begin to write whatever comes to mind, without overthinking or editing. Trust your intuition to guide your words.

After a few minutes, review what you've written and look for any intuitive insights or guidance.

Chakra Meditation:

Chakras are energy centers in the body associated with different aspects of life. Intuition is often linked to the Third Eye chakra, located in the forehead.

Find a quiet space to sit or lie down.

Close your eyes and take several deep breaths.

Focus your attention on the area between your eyebrows (the location of the Third Eye chakra).

Imagine a deep indigo or purple light in this area, and visualize it expanding and becoming brighter with each breath.

As you meditate on the Third Eye, pay attention to any insights or feelings that arise.

Nature Meditation:

Find a peaceful outdoor spot, like a park or garden.

Sit comfortably or take a leisurely walk.

Connect with the natural surroundings, focusing on the sights, sounds, and sensations.

As you immerse yourself in nature, let your intuition guide you and see if it offers any insights or messages related to your questions or concerns.

Remember that intuition often speaks softly and subtly. Be patient and open-minded during your meditation practices, and don't force any insights to come. Over time, regular meditation can help you become more attuned to your intuitive wisdom.

Challenges and Growth

Challenges and growth are closely interconnected aspects of human life. Challenges, whether personal, professional, or emotional, often provide opportunities for growth and development. Here's a more detailed exploration of this relationship:

Personal Growth Through Challenges:

Challenges force us out of our comfort zones: When we face challenges, we are compelled to confront new situations, problems, or experiences that we may not have encountered otherwise. This can lead to personal growth as we learn to adapt and navigate unfamiliar terrain.

Resilience and problem-solving skills: Challenges can teach us resilience, the ability to bounce back from adversity, and problem-solving skills. When we overcome difficulties, we gain confidence in our abilities to handle future challenges.

Self-discovery: Challenges often reveal our strengths, weaknesses, and inner resources. They provide opportunities for self-discovery and self-awareness, allowing us to understand ourselves better and work on personal development.

Learning and knowledge: Overcoming challenges often involves acquiring new knowledge and skills. Whether it's learning from mistakes or seeking solutions to problems, challenges can be valuable learning experiences.

Professional Growth Through Challenges:

Skill development: Professional challenges, such as new projects or responsibilities, can help us develop and refine our skills. These challenges can push us to expand our knowledge and expertise in our chosen field.

Leadership and adaptability: Navigating challenges in the workplace can improve leadership abilities and adaptability. Leaders often emerge when they are tested, and adaptability is a highly valued skill in today's rapidly changing work environment.

Networking and collaboration: Challenges can also foster collaboration and networking as individuals and teams work together to find solutions. Building these relationships can be instrumental in career growth.

Career advancement: Successfully overcoming workplace challenges can lead to career advancement opportunities. Employers often recognize and reward individuals who demonstrate the ability to handle difficult situations effectively.

Emotional and Psychological Growth Through Challenges:

Resilience and emotional intelligence: Emotional challenges, such as coping with loss or adversity, can foster emotional resilience and enhance emotional intelligence. These experiences can deepen our understanding of our own emotions and the emotions of others.

Empathy and compassion: Overcoming personal hardships can make us more empathetic and compassionate toward others who are facing similar challenges. This can strengthen our relationships and our ability to support others.

Perspective and gratitude: Facing significant challenges can shift our perspective on life. We may come to appreciate the value of what we have and cultivate gratitude for the positive aspects of our lives.

Personal transformation: Some challenges can lead to profound personal transformations. People often emerge from difficult experiences with a changed outlook on life, revised priorities, and a greater sense of purpose.

In conclusion, while challenges can be demanding and uncomfortable, they are also opportunities for growth, learning, and transformation. Embracing challenges with a positive mindset, resilience, and a willingness to learn can lead to personal, professional, and emotional development. Challenges are not obstacles to growth but rather stepping stones on the path to becoming the best version of ourselves.

Dealing with distractions is a common challenge, especially in today's fast-paced, technology-driven world. Whether you're trying to focus on work, study, or any important task, managing distractions is crucial for productivity and efficiency. Here are some strategies to help you effectively deal with distractions:

Create a Distraction-Free Environment:

> **Designated workspace:** Set up a specific area where you work or study. Make sure it's organized, comfortable, and free from unnecessary distractions.

> **Minimize noise:** Use noise-canceling headphones or play background music (instrumental or calming) to block out distractions from noise.

> **Limit access to distractions:** Keep your phone, social media, or other distracting devices out of sight and reach while you work.

Set Clear Goals and Priorities:

> **Task prioritization:** Make a to-do list or schedule for the day, setting clear priorities for what needs to be accomplished.

> **Break tasks into manageable chunks:** Divide larger tasks into smaller, achievable parts. This makes it easier to stay focused and reduces overwhelm.

> **Time blocking:** Allocate specific blocks of time to different tasks. During these blocks, focus solely on the task at hand and avoid distractions.

Practice Mindfulness:

Mindful awareness: Develop mindfulness techniques to bring your attention back to the present moment whenever you notice your mind wandering.

Breathing exercises: Incorporate simple breathing exercises to help you stay centered and focused.

Implement Time Management Techniques:

Pomodoro Technique: Work for a set time (e.g., 25 minutes) and then take a short break. Repeat this cycle to maintain productivity.

Time tracking: Use a timer to track your work sessions and breaks. Knowing how much time you're spending on tasks can increase awareness and productivity.

Practice Self-Discipline:

Set clear rules and boundaries: Establish rules for yourself, such as no social media during work hours, and stick to them.

Delay gratification: Reward yourself with a break or a specific activity only after completing a task or reaching a milestone.

Address Physical Well-Being:

Adequate rest and sleep: Ensure you're getting enough quality sleep to maintain focus and concentration during the day.

Healthy diet: Eat nutritious meals and stay hydrated, as a well-nourished body and brain can help reduce distractions.

Manage Digital Distractions:

Notifications and alerts: Turn off non-essential notifications on your devices to avoid constant interruptions.

Designated communication times: Set specific times to check emails, messages, or social media, rather than responding to them immediately.

Practice Discipline in Technology Use:

App usage control: Use apps or features that limit the time you spend on distracting websites or apps.

Digital detox: Consider occasional digital detox periods where you disconnect from technology to rejuvenate your focus and creativity.

Seek Accountability and Support:

Accountability partner: Share your goals and progress with a trusted friend or colleague who can hold you accountable and provide encouragement.

Join a focused group: Participate in group activities or coworking sessions where everyone is working on their tasks, creating a conducive atmosphere for focus.

Practice Patience and Persistence:

Be patient with yourself: Changing habits and managing distractions takes time and effort. Celebrate your progress and keep refining your strategies.

Learn from distractions: Understand what triggers your distractions and use this knowledge to develop better strategies for the future.

Remember, managing distractions is an ongoing practice that requires dedication and adaptability. By implementing these strategies consistently and adjusting them to suit your needs, you can enhance your ability to stay focused and productive amidst various distractions

Impatience and frustration are common emotions that everyone experiences from time to time. These emotions can arise in various situations, such as when facing delays, obstacles, or unmet expectations. While they are normal reactions, excessive impatience and frustration can negatively affect your well-being and relationships. Here are some strategies to help you manage impatience and frustration effectively:

Identify Triggers: Recognize the situations, people, or circumstances that tend to trigger impatience and frustration in your life. By understanding your triggers, you can be more prepared to manage these emotions when they arise.

Practice Mindfulness: Mindfulness involves being fully present in the moment without judgment. When you feel impatience or frustration building, take a moment to focus on your breath and ground yourself in the present. This can help you regain perspective and prevent these emotions from escalating.

Reframe Your Thoughts: Challenge negative or irrational thoughts that contribute to impatience and frustration. Ask yourself if your expectations are realistic or if there's a more positive way to view the situation.

Replace catastrophic thinking with more balanced and constructive thoughts. For example, instead of thinking, "This is a disaster," try, "This is a challenge, but I can handle it."

Develop Emotional Awareness: Pay attention to your emotional state and physical sensations when you start to feel impatient or frustrated. Recognize the early signs, such as muscle tension or racing thoughts, and use this awareness to intervene before these emotions intensify.

Practice Deep Breathing: Deep, slow breaths can help calm your nervous system and reduce the intensity of impatience and frustration. Take a few deep breaths in through your nose, hold for a moment, and then exhale slowly through your mouth.

Take Breaks: If you're feeling overwhelmed by impatience or frustration, step away from the situation if possible. A short break can provide you with the space to cool down and gain perspective.

Problem-Solve: Instead of dwelling on what's frustrating you, focus on finding solutions. Identify actionable steps you can take to address the situation or work towards your goals.

Set Realistic Expectations: Adjust your expectations to be more realistic and flexible. Understand that not everything will go as planned, and delays or obstacles are a part of life.

Practice Patience-Building Activities: Engage in activities that naturally cultivate patience, such as meditation, yoga, or mindfulness exercises. These practices can help you develop a greater tolerance for uncertainty and frustration.

Seek Support: Talk to a trusted friend, family member, or therapist about your feelings of impatience and frustration. Sometimes, discussing your emotions with someone who listens non-judgmentally can provide relief and perspective.

Learn from Your Experiences: Reflect on past situations where impatience or frustration got the best of you. What did you learn from those experiences? Use those lessons to improve your emotional response in the future.

Remember that managing impatience and frustration is an ongoing process. It's normal to experience these emotions, but with practice and self-awareness, you can develop healthier coping mechanisms and responses. Ultimately, the goal is to maintain emotional balance and resilience in the face of life's challenges

Consistency and motivation are key factors in achieving long-term goals, maintaining positive habits, and sustaining personal growth.

However, they can be challenging to maintain over time. Here are some strategies to help you stay consistent and motivated in pursuing your goals:

Set Clear and Specific Goals: Clearly define your goals with specific details. Having a clear target makes it easier to stay motivated and measure your progress.

Break Goals into Smaller Steps: Divide your larger goals into smaller, manageable tasks. This makes the process less overwhelming and allows you to celebrate small victories along the way.

Create a Plan: Develop a structured plan or schedule that outlines how you will work towards your goals. Knowing what you need to do each day or week keeps you on track.

Establish a Routine: Consistency often thrives in routines. Set aside dedicated times each day or week for working on your goals. Over time, this can become a habit that requires less effort to maintain.

Find Intrinsic Motivation: Identify why your goals matter to you on a personal level. Connecting your goals to your values and passions can provide a strong intrinsic motivation to keep going.

Visualize Success: Use visualization techniques to imagine yourself successfully achieving your goals. This mental imagery can boost motivation and create a positive mindset.

Stay Accountable: Share your goals with a friend, family member, or a mentor who can help hold you accountable. Regular check-ins and support can help maintain motivation.

Use Positive Reinforcement: Reward yourself for achieving milestones and staying consistent. Rewards can serve as positive reinforcement to keep you motivated.

Focus on Progress, Not Perfection: Understand that perfection is not necessary. Consistency is about making progress, even if it's slow. Embrace the learning process and don't be too hard on yourself when setbacks occur.

Stay Inspired: Continuously seek inspiration and new ideas related to your goals. Reading, attending seminars, or connecting with like-minded individuals can reignite your motivation.

Overcome Obstacles: Anticipate and plan for obstacles that may arise. Having strategies in place to deal with setbacks can help you stay consistent even when challenges occur.

Cultivate Self-Discipline: Develop self-discipline by practicing restraint and delayed gratification. Discipline can help you stick to your plan even when motivation wanes.

Track Your Progress: Keep a journal or use a tracking app to monitor your progress. Seeing how far you've come can provide a sense of accomplishment and motivation.

Embrace Change and Adapt: Be open to adjusting your goals or strategies as needed. Sometimes, what worked initially may need to evolve over time.

Surround Yourself with Positivity: Surround yourself with people, environments, and influences that support your goals and maintain your motivation.

Remember that motivation can fluctuate, but it's your commitment to consistency that often leads to long-term success. Cultivating these habits and strategies can help you maintain your motivation and achieve your goals over time

Meditation is often referred to as a powerful tool for healing, both in the physical and emotional sense. While meditation is not a substitute for medical treatment, it can complement conventional therapies and contribute to overall well-being. Here are ways in which meditation can harness its healing power:

Stress Reduction: One of the most widely recognized benefits of meditation is its ability to reduce stress. Through mindfulness meditation and deep breathing exercises, individuals can activate the body's relaxation response, which lowers stress hormones like cortisol.

Anxiety and Depression Management: Regular meditation practices have been shown to reduce symptoms of anxiety and depression. Meditation helps individuals gain better control over their thoughts and emotions, promoting a sense of calm and inner peace.

Pain Management: Meditation can assist in pain management by changing one's perception of pain and enhancing pain tolerance. It can also lead to the release of endorphins, the body's natural painkillers.

Improved Sleep Quality: Insomnia and sleep disorders can be alleviated through meditation. Relaxation techniques and mindfulness can calm the mind and reduce racing thoughts, making it easier to fall asleep and stay asleep.

Enhanced Immune Function: Meditation has been linked to improved immune system function. A reduction in stress hormones and increased relaxation response may contribute to better immune health.

Lower Blood Pressure: Meditation, particularly mindfulness meditation, can have a positive impact on blood pressure. It helps relax the blood vessels and reduces tension, contributing to lower blood pressure levels.

Emotional Healing: Meditation allows individuals to process and release suppressed emotions. It provides a safe space for acknowledging and understanding past traumas or emotional wounds.

Increased Self-Awareness: Meditation fosters self-awareness by encouraging individuals to observe their thoughts and emotions without judgment. This self-awareness can lead to better emotional regulation and healthier decision-making.

Improved Focus and Concentration: Meditation practices that involve concentration techniques can enhance focus and concentration. This can be particularly beneficial for individuals with attention-related disorders.

Better Coping with Chronic Illness: People dealing with chronic illnesses often find solace in meditation. It can improve their mental and emotional well-being, relieve pain, and enhance their overall quality of life.

Greater Resilience: Regular meditation can help individuals build resilience to life's challenges. It equips them with coping strategies and a more balanced perspective on difficulties.

Spiritual Growth and Connection: For some, meditation is a means of connecting with a higher power, fostering spiritual growth, and gaining a sense of purpose and meaning in life.

Enhanced Mind-Body Connection: Meditation can help individuals become more attuned to their bodies and better understand their physical and emotional needs.

It's important to note that the healing power of meditation may vary from person to person. What works for one individual may not work the same way for another. Additionally, meditation is most effective when practiced regularly and consistently over time.

If you're considering incorporating meditation into your healing journey, it's advisable to consult with a healthcare professional or seek guidance from a qualified meditation teacher or therapist. They can help you tailor a meditation practice that suits your specific needs and circumstances.

Stress reduction and relaxation techniques are essential tools for managing the challenges of modern life and maintaining overall well-being. Here are various techniques and practices you can use to reduce stress and promote relaxation:

Deep Breathing Exercises: Deep breathing is a simple yet highly effective technique for reducing stress and promoting relaxation. It can help calm the nervous system and reduce the production of stress hormones like cortisol.

Try the 4-7-8 technique: Inhale deeply through your nose for a count of 4, hold your breath for a count of 7, and exhale slowly through your mouth for a count of 8.

Progressive Muscle Relaxation (PMR): PMR involves tensing and then relaxing different muscle groups to release physical tension. It's an excellent way to relax your body.

Start with your toes and work your way up to your head, focusing on each muscle group as you go.

Mindfulness Meditation: Mindfulness meditation involves paying non-judgmental attention to the present moment. It can help you become more aware of your thoughts and feelings, reducing stress and anxiety.

Focus on your breath, bodily sensations, or a specific meditation object. When your mind wanders, gently bring your attention back.

Yoga: Yoga combines physical postures, deep breathing, and meditation to promote relaxation, flexibility, and stress reduction.

Regular yoga practice can help reduce muscle tension and improve overall well-being.

Guided Imagery and Visualization: Guided imagery involves using your imagination to create a peaceful and calming mental image. Visualization exercises can help you relax and reduce stress.

Close your eyes and imagine a place or scenario that brings you comfort and relaxation, such as a beach, forest, or peaceful garden.

Autogenic Training: Autogenic training is a relaxation technique that focuses on achieving a state of physical and mental relaxation through self-suggestion and imagery.

It involves repeating a series of phrases or affirmations related to warmth, heaviness, and relaxation in different parts of your body.

Tai Chi: Tai Chi is a mind-body practice that combines slow, flowing movements with deep breathing and meditation. It's particularly effective for reducing stress and improving balance and flexibility.

Aromatherapy: Aromatherapy involves using essential oils, such as lavender, chamomile, or eucalyptus, to promote relaxation and reduce stress.

You can use essential oils in a diffuser, add a few drops to a warm bath, or apply diluted oils to your skin.

Exercise: Regular physical activity, such as jogging, swimming, or dancing, can reduce stress by increasing the production of endorphins, which are natural mood lifters.

Progressive Relaxation Apps and Audio: There are many apps and audio recordings available that guide you through relaxation and stress reduction exercises. These resources can be convenient for daily practice.

Journaling: Keeping a journal can help you process and manage stress. Write down your thoughts, feelings, and concerns to gain clarity and reduce emotional tension.

Disconnect from Screens: Reduce screen time, especially before bedtime. The blue light emitted by screens can interfere with your sleep patterns and contribute to stress.

Spend Time in Nature: Spending time outdoors in natural settings can have a calming and rejuvenating effect on your mind and body.

Remember that relaxation techniques are personal, and what works best for one person may not work as effectively for another.

Experiment with different techniques to find what resonates and integrates well into your daily life. Consistent practice is key to reaping the full benefits of stress reduction and relaxation techniques

Coping with trauma and pain can be an incredibly challenging and deeply personal journey. Trauma can manifest in many forms, such as physical, emotional, or psychological, and it often brings with it physical and emotional pain. Here are some strategies and approaches to help cope with trauma and pain:

Seek Professional Help: Reach out to a therapist, counselor, or psychologist who specializes in trauma and pain management. Professional guidance can provide you with the tools and support you need to navigate your healing journey.

Build a Support System: Connect with friends and family members you trust. Sharing your experiences and feelings with loved ones can be comforting and provide emotional support.

Practice Self-Care: Prioritize self-care to nurture your physical and emotional well-being. This can include maintaining a balanced diet, getting regular exercise, and ensuring you get enough sleep.

Mindfulness and Meditation: Mindfulness and meditation techniques can help you become more aware of your thoughts and emotions, providing a means to manage them in a healthier way. Mindfulness can also help you stay grounded in the present moment.

Therapy Modalities: Explore therapy modalities that are known to be effective in trauma recovery, such as Eye Movement Desensitization and Reprocessing (EMDR), Cognitive-Behavioral Therapy (CBT), or Dialectical Behavior Therapy (DBT).

Art and Creative Expression: Engage in creative activities such as art, music, or writing. Expressing your emotions through these mediums can be therapeutic and help you process trauma and pain.

Support Groups: Consider joining a support group for trauma survivors. Being in a group of people who have had similar experiences can provide validation, understanding, and a sense of community.

Self-Compassion: Practice self-compassion by treating yourself with kindness and understanding. Avoid self-blame and judgment, recognizing that healing takes time.

Set Boundaries: Establish clear boundaries in your life to protect your emotional and physical well-being. Learn to say "no" when necessary and prioritize your needs.

Relaxation Techniques: Incorporate relaxation techniques such as deep breathing, progressive muscle relaxation, or guided imagery to manage physical and emotional pain.

Journaling: Keep a journal to document your thoughts and feelings. Writing can help you gain insight, process emotions, and track your progress.

Safety and Self-Care Plans: Develop safety plans for times when you may feel overwhelmed or unsafe. Have a list of activities or people you can turn to for support during difficult moments.

Professional Pain Management: If you are dealing with physical pain, consult with a healthcare provider for pain management strategies, which may include medication, physical therapy, or alternative therapies.

Patience and Persistence: Recognize that healing from trauma and pain is a gradual process. Be patient with yourself and understand that setbacks are a natural part of the journey.

Focus on Resilience: Acknowledge your resilience and inner strength. Celebrate your ability to survive and thrive despite the challenges you've faced.

It's important to remember that healing from trauma and pain is not linear, and everyone's journey is unique. What works for one person may not work the same way for another. Seek professional help when needed, and don't hesitate to reach out to a therapist or counselor who can provide personalized guidance and support tailored to your specific needs. Healing is possible, and with time and effort, you can find relief and regain a sense of well-being.

Integration and transformation are two interrelated processes often associated with personal growth, healing, and development. They involve making sense of experiences, applying newfound insights, and evolving into a more authentic and resilient version of oneself. Here's a closer look at both concepts:

Integration: Integration involves bringing together different aspects of oneself or various experiences into a harmonious and cohesive whole. It's a process of unifying fragmented parts of your identity, emotions, or knowledge. Integration can apply to various areas of life:

Emotional Integration: This refers to accepting and processing all emotions, even difficult ones like anger, sadness, or fear, rather than suppressing or denying them. Emotional integration allows you to be more in touch with your feelings and respond to them in a healthy way.

Identity Integration: This is about embracing all aspects of your identity, including your strengths and weaknesses, past experiences, cultural background, and values. It involves self-acceptance and recognizing that your identity is multifaceted.

Trauma Integration: Trauma integration is the process of healing from past traumas and incorporating the lessons learned into your life. It allows you to move forward with a deeper understanding of yourself and your resilience.

Knowledge Integration: In learning and personal development, knowledge integration involves synthesizing information and experiences to create a more comprehensive understanding of a subject or situation.

Transformation: Transformation is a profound and often radical change that goes beyond mere adjustment or adaptation. It's a process of fundamental change in how you perceive, think, feel, and behave. Here are some contexts in which transformation can occur:

Personal Growth: Transformation often accompanies personal growth. It can involve a shift in mindset, beliefs, or values that leads to a more authentic and fulfilling life.

Healing: Trauma or challenging life experiences can lead to transformation as individuals work through their pain and emerge stronger, with a deeper sense of purpose and resilience.

Spiritual Awakening: Some people experience spiritual transformation, which may involve a shift in their understanding of existence, a connection to a higher power, or a deepening of their spiritual practices.

Career and Lifestyle: A career or lifestyle transformation might involve a significant change in one's profession, life goals, or daily routines to align better with one's values and passions.

Relationships: Transformative changes can occur in relationships, such as moving from conflict and dysfunction to greater understanding and harmony.

Integration and Transformation Together: Integration and transformation often go hand in hand. The process of transformation often requires integration to fully absorb and apply the lessons and changes that result from a transformative experience. For example:

After a healing journey from trauma (transformation), integration allows you to incorporate the newfound resilience and self-understanding into your daily life.

Following a personal growth or spiritual awakening (transformation), integration helps you align your beliefs and values with your actions and decisions.

Both integration and transformation are ongoing processes that can happen multiple times in a person's life. They require self-awareness, reflection, and sometimes external support, such as therapy or counseling, to navigate effectively. Embracing these processes can lead to personal fulfillment, emotional well-being, and a more authentic and meaningful life.

Bringing meditation into your daily life can be a transformative practice that enhances your overall well-being, reduces stress, and cultivates mindfulness. Here are practical tips to help you incorporate meditation seamlessly into your routine:

Start with Short Sessions: Begin with brief meditation sessions, such as 5-10 minutes. Shorter sessions are more manageable for beginners and can be easily integrated into your daily schedule.

Choose a Consistent Time: Select a specific time each day for meditation. Whether it's in the morning, during lunch, or before bedtime, consistency helps establish a routine.

Create a Dedicated Space: Set up a designated meditation space that is quiet and free from distractions. Over time, this space will become associated with mindfulness and relaxation.

Set Realistic Goals: Avoid setting lofty meditation goals initially. Instead, aim for consistency. Gradually increase the duration and complexity of your practice as it becomes a habit.

Incorporate Mindful Moments: Infuse mindfulness into daily activities. Practice mindfulness while eating, walking, or doing household chores by focusing on the sensations and experiences in the present moment.

Use Meditation Apps or Guided Sessions: Utilize meditation apps or guided sessions to structure your practice. There are various apps available with guided meditations tailored to different needs and time constraints.

Mindful Breathing Breaks: Take short mindful breathing breaks throughout the day. Pause for a minute or two to focus on your breath and center yourself, especially during moments of stress or agitation.

Mindful Transitions: Practice mindfulness during transitions between activities. Before starting a new task, take a moment to ground yourself and set a clear intention for what you're about to do.

Use Reminders: Set alarms or reminders on your phone or computer to prompt you to take meditation breaks. This can help maintain consistency.

Journaling: After your meditation sessions, consider journaling about your experiences, insights, or any challenges you faced. Journaling can deepen your self-awareness and understanding of your meditation practice.

Join a Group or Class: Consider joining a meditation group or class. The sense of community and shared practice can provide motivation and accountability.

Be Kind to Yourself: Understand that your meditation practice will have ups and downs. If you miss a session or find it challenging, be gentle with yourself and return to your practice without judgment.

Experiment with Different Techniques: Explore various meditation techniques, such as mindfulness meditation, loving-kindness meditation, or body scan meditation, to find what resonates with you.

Reflect on Benefits: Regularly reflect on the benefits of your meditation practice. Notice how it affects your mood, stress levels, and overall well-being. This reinforcement can motivate you to continue.

Combine Meditation with Other Habits: Link meditation with other daily routines, such as brushing your teeth or making your morning coffee. Over time, these associations can make meditation feel like a natural part of your day.

Remember that meditation is a personal practice, and there's no one-size-fits-all approach. The key is to find a rhythm and routine that aligns with your lifestyle and preferences. Over time, with patience and persistence, meditation can become an integral and enriching part of your daily life.

Incorporating mindfulness into routine activities is a powerful way to bring greater presence, awareness, and peace into your daily life. Here are some practical tips for infusing mindfulness into your everyday activities:

Start with Intention: Begin each day with the intention to be mindful. Set a clear intention to stay present and fully engage with your daily activities.

Mindful Morning Routine: Pay close attention to your morning routine, such as brushing your teeth, taking a shower, or making breakfast. Notice the sensations, smells, and sounds as you go about these tasks.

Mindful Eating: When you eat, savor each bite. Pay attention to the taste, texture, and smell of your food. Eat slowly and chew your food thoroughly.

Walking Meditation: Practice walking meditation when you're moving from one place to another. Feel each step, notice your breath, and observe your surroundings as you walk mindfully.

Mindful Breathing Breaks: Take short mindful breathing breaks throughout the day. Pause for a minute or two to focus on your breath and bring your awareness to the present moment.

Mindful Listening: Practice active listening during conversations. Give your full attention to the speaker, without thinking about what you'll say next. This fosters deeper connections and understanding.

Mindful Commuting: Whether you're driving or taking public transportation, use your commute as an opportunity for mindfulness. Pay attention to the road or your surroundings, and avoid distractions.

Mindful Waiting: Use moments of waiting, such as standing in line or waiting for an appointment, as opportunities for mindfulness. Focus on your breath or the sensations in your body.

Mindful Technology Use: Be mindful of your technology use. Set aside specific times to check emails and social media rather than constantly reacting to notifications.

Mindful Cleaning and Chores: Approach household chores and cleaning mindfully. Focus on the task at hand, the sensations of cleaning, and the sense of accomplishment as you complete each chore.

Mindful Driving or Commuting: While driving or commuting, be fully present on the road. Notice your surroundings, the feel of the steering wheel or handlebars, and your breath as you drive.

Mindful Work: Bring mindfulness to your work by fully engaging in your tasks. Minimize distractions and immerse yourself in the task at hand.

Mindful Breaks: Take short mindful breaks during your workday. Stand up, stretch, and take a few deep breaths to refresh your mind and reduce stress.

Mindful Evening Routine: Wind down your day with a mindful evening routine. Reflect on the events of the day, express gratitude, and prepare your mind for restful sleep.

Mindful Bedtime: As you prepare for sleep, be mindful of the sensations and comfort of your bed. Practice relaxation techniques or a brief meditation to ease into a peaceful sleep.

Remember that mindfulness is a skill that develops with practice. Be patient with yourself and approach each activity with curiosity and non-judgment. Over time, incorporating mindfulness into routine activities can enhance your overall sense of well-being and help you find greater joy and presence in each moment of your life

Living a more conscious and intentional life involves making deliberate choices, being fully present in each moment, and aligning your actions with your values and goals. Here are steps you can take to cultivate a more conscious and intentional way of living:

Clarify Your Values: Begin by identifying your core values—what matters most to you in life. Your values serve as a compass to guide your decisions and actions.

Set Clear Intentions: Define your intentions for different areas of your life, such as relationships, career, health, and personal growth. Intentions are like roadmaps that help you stay on course.

Mindfulness Practice: Develop a regular mindfulness practice, such as meditation or mindful breathing. Mindfulness enhances your awareness of the present moment and allows you to make more conscious choices.

Practice Gratitude: Cultivate gratitude by reflecting on the positive aspects of your life. This helps you appreciate what you have and fosters a positive outlook.

Eliminate Distractions: Identify and minimize distractions in your life, especially those that take you away from your goals and values. This might involve reducing screen time, decluttering your physical space, or setting boundaries with time-consuming activities.

Set Priorities: Determine your top priorities in various areas of your life. Focus your time and energy on what matters most, rather than spreading yourself too thin.

Daily Reflection: Dedicate time each day for reflection. Review your goals, intentions, and actions. Ask yourself if your choices align with your values and if adjustments are needed.

Practice Mindful Decision-Making: Before making decisions, pause and reflect on how each choice aligns with your values and intentions. Avoid impulsive or automatic decisions.

Simplify Your Life: Simplify your daily routines and commitments. A simpler life often allows for more intentional living and greater focus on what truly matters.

Set Boundaries: Establish clear boundaries in your relationships and commitments. Boundaries protect your time, energy, and well-being.

Self-Care: Prioritize self-care and self-compassion. Taking care of yourself is essential for maintaining the physical and emotional resources needed for intentional living.

Practice Mindful Communication: Engage in mindful and empathetic communication with others. Listen actively, speak consciously, and choose your words carefully.

Learn Continuously: Cultivate a growth mindset and a hunger for learning. Seek new knowledge and experiences that align with your values and interests.

Journaling: Keep a journal to record your thoughts, feelings, and experiences. Journaling can help you gain clarity and insight into your life.

Celebrate Progress: Acknowledge and celebrate your achievements and progress, no matter how small. This reinforces your commitment to intentional living.

Embrace Flexibility: While intentionality is important, remain open to change and adapt when necessary. Life is dynamic, and your goals and values may evolve.

Connect with a Supportive Community: Surround yourself with people who share your values and support your intentional living journey. Community can provide encouragement and accountability.

Living a conscious and intentional life is an ongoing practice that requires mindfulness, self-reflection, and a commitment to aligning your actions with your values and intentions. Over time, this approach can lead to a deeper sense of purpose, fulfillment, and well-being

The journey of self-discovery is a lifelong and often endless process of learning, growth, and self-awareness. It involves exploring your inner self, understanding your values, beliefs, emotions, and motivations, and continuously evolving as a person. Here are some key aspects of the endless journey of self-discovery:

Self-Awareness: Self-discovery begins with self-awareness. It's the ability to observe your thoughts, emotions, and behaviors without judgment. Through self-awareness, you gain insights into your patterns, strengths, weaknesses, and areas for growth.

Reflection: Regular self-reflection is essential for self-discovery. Take time to contemplate your experiences, relationships, and choices. Journaling can be a valuable tool for introspection.

Embracing Change: As you learn more about yourself, you may realize that you are not static. You change and evolve over time. Embrace change as a natural part of your self-discovery journey.

Facing Challenges: Self-discovery often involves confronting challenges, both internal and external. These challenges can be opportunities for growth and self-understanding.

Exploring Passions and Interests: To know yourself better, explore your passions, interests, and curiosities. Engaging in activities you love can reveal new facets of your personality.

Seeking Feedback: Solicit feedback from trusted friends, family, mentors, and even professionals. Others may provide insights about your blind spots and areas where you can grow.

Questioning Beliefs: Be open to questioning your beliefs and assumptions. Sometimes, deeply held beliefs may limit your self-discovery. Consider alternative perspectives.

Mindfulness and Meditation: Mindfulness practices, such as meditation, can help you become more attuned to your thoughts, feelings, and bodily sensations. They promote self-awareness and self-acceptance.

Self-Compassion: Treat yourself with kindness and compassion. Self-discovery can bring up challenging emotions and realizations. Practicing self-compassion helps you navigate these moments with gentleness.

Acceptance: Acceptance of who you are at each stage of your self-discovery journey is crucial. You are a complex and ever-changing individual, and self-acceptance is a cornerstone of growth.

Setting Goals: Establish personal and developmental goals that align with your values and aspirations. Goals can provide direction and motivation in your journey.

Learning from Mistakes: Embrace mistakes and failures as opportunities for learning and growth. They can reveal important insights about your values and priorities.

Cultivating Relationships: Interactions with others can be mirrors that reflect aspects of yourself. Building and maintaining healthy relationships can aid in self-discovery.

Seeking Meaning and Purpose: Explore questions of meaning and purpose in your life. What brings you fulfillment, and how can you align your actions with your sense of purpose?

Transcending Ego: Self-discovery often involves transcending the ego, letting go of attachments to self-image and societal expectations, and connecting with a deeper sense of self.

Continuous Learning: Approach self-discovery with a sense of curiosity and a commitment to continuous learning. There is always more to uncover about yourself.

The journey of self-discovery is unique to each individual, and there is no endpoint or final destination. It's a process of continual exploration, growth, and evolution. Embrace the journey with an open heart and a willingness to embrace the ever-unfolding layers of your inner self. It's a journey that can bring you greater self-awareness, inner peace, and a deeper connection with the world around you.

Exploring meditation and deepening your practice can be a rewarding journey. There are numerous resources available to support your meditation practice and further exploration of mindfulness and self-awareness. Here are some valuable resources to consider:

Meditation Apps:

Headspace: Offers guided meditation sessions and mindfulness exercises.

Calm: Provides guided meditations, sleep stories, and relaxation techniques.

Insight Timer: Offers a vast library of free meditations, music, and talks by meditation teachers from around the world.

10% Happier: Features meditation courses, guided practices, and interviews with meditation experts.

Online Courses and Programs:

Mindfulness-Based Stress Reduction (MBSR): An evidence-based program developed by Jon Kabat-Zinn that teaches mindfulness meditation to reduce stress and enhance well-being. You can find MBSR courses online and in-person.

Mindful Schools: Offers online courses and programs focused on teaching mindfulness and meditation to children, adolescents, and adults.

Coursera and edX: Platforms that provide courses on mindfulness and meditation from universities and institutions around the world.

YouTube Channels and Guided Meditations:

The Honest Guys: Offers a wide range of guided meditations and relaxation videos.

Yoga with Adriene: Includes yoga and meditation practices for various levels and needs.

Tara Brach: Features guided meditations and talks on mindfulness, compassion, and self-acceptance.

Meditation Retreats and Workshops:

Explore local or virtual meditation retreats, workshops, and classes led by experienced meditation teachers or organizations. Retreats can offer immersive experiences and opportunities for deepening your practice.

Podcasts:

On Being with Krista Tippett: Features interviews with spiritual and mindfulness leaders, exploring themes of inner life and self-awareness.

The Daily Meditation Podcast: Offers daily guided meditations and mindfulness practices.

Local Meditation Centers:

Research meditation centers, yoga studios, or mindfulness groups in your area. Many communities offer group meditation sessions and teachings.

Mindfulness-Based Books and Courses for Specific Issues:

If you're interested in mindfulness for specific issues like anxiety, depression, or chronic pain, consider resources tailored to these areas. For example, "The Mindful Way Through Depression" by Mark Williams and others is a book and program focused on mindfulness for depression.

Online Forums and Communities:

Connect with like-minded individuals on meditation and mindfulness forums, such as those on Reddit, and engage in discussions, ask questions, and share experiences.

Meditation Retreat Centers: If you're interested in deepening your practice through longer retreats, consider attending retreat centers like the Insight Meditation Society (IMS), Spirit Rock, or the Shambhala Mountain Center, which offer various meditation retreats and programs.

Remember that the resources you choose should align with your goals and preferences. Whether you're a beginner looking to start a meditation practice or an experienced meditator seeking to deepen your understanding, these resources can help you on your journey of self-discovery and mindfulness.

About the Author

Evangeline Brooks is a contemplative thinker and writer whose work delves into the philosophy of joy and existence. Following her well-received debut, "The Art of Being Happy: A Philosophical Exploration," Brooks continues her exploration of inner well-being with her second book. She intertwines her rich knowledge of meditation with practical insights, drawing from a diverse spectrum of cultural and historical contexts. Her writing is not only informative but also deeply transformative, as she encourages readers to embark on a journey towards self-discovery and the untapped potential within. Brooks's voice is a beacon for those navigating the complex voyage of finding peace and authenticity in the modern world.